THE BIBLE AND THE MASS

The Bible and the Mass

Understanding the Scriptural Basis of the Liturgy

Reverend Peter M.J. Stravinskas

REDEEMER BOOKS

Servant Publications
Ann Arbor, Michigan

Published by Servant Publications
P.O. Box 8617
Ann Arbor, Michigan 48107

Redeemer Books is an imprint of Servant Publications especially
designed to serve Roman Catholics.

Published with the ecclesiastical approval of The Most Reverend Paul
A. Baltakis, OFM, Bishop for the Spiritual Assistance of Lithuanians
Outside Lithuania.

Cover design by Robert Coe & Charles Piccirilli
Cover photo by Lawrence Fitton

Printed in the United States of America

92 93 10 9 8 7 6 5 4 3

ISBN 0-89283-628-8

Library of Congress Cataloging-in-Publication Data

Stravinskas, Peter M.J.
  The Bible and the Mass / understanding the scriptural basis of the
  liturgy / by Peter M.J. Stravinskas.
    p.   cm.
  "A Redeemer book."
  ISBN 0-89283-628-8
  1. Mass.   2. Lord's Supper (Liturgy)   3. Catholic Church—
Liturgy.   I. Title.
BX2015.S77   1989
264'.02036—dc20   89-27773
                                                            CIP

Dedication

To Nicholas Gregoris, my son in the Lord,
whose love for the liturgy
is such an inspiration
and whose collaboration in this project
was so helpful.

May his studies for the priesthood
now beginning
lead him *usque ad sacra mysteria celebranda.*

Contents

Acknowledgments

Some of the scriptural meditations at the end of each chapter are taken from the author's *Prayerbook of the Bible*, published by Our Sunday Visitor, Inc., copyright © 1984 by Our Sunday Visitor Publishing Division, Our Sunday Visitor, Inc. All rights reserved. Used by permission of the publisher.

Substantial portions of the reflections on the four Eucharistic Prayers originally appeared in a series in 1987 on that topic in the *National Catholic Register*.

The author notes with gratitude the assistance and suggestions of Fathers Peter Scagnelli, Perry Dodds, Michael Davino, and Giles Dimock, whose insights, encouragement, and support were invaluable.

Publisher's Preface

The Bible and the Mass is intended to help you under-stand the scriptural and historical origins of the prayers used in the Mass—from the Introductory Rites to the Concluding Rite. In this book, which is formatted for use by both individuals and groups, Fr. Peter Stravinskas explains the various rites of the Mass and even includes separate essays on each of the four Eucharistic Prayers. At the end of all four chapters, a week of scriptural meditations and five questions for group discussion enable you to meditate on key Scrip-tures pertinent to the rites just studied and then to meet with others for group discussion.

The purpose of this book, however, is not simply to understand better the various prayers for the rites of the Mass, but also to participate more fully in the celebration of the Mass. Therefore, your study and meditation during the week should lead to greater participation in Sunday and weekday Mass. This might be best accomplished if you focus on participating in the rite currently under study when next you attend Mass.

At points throughout *The Bible and the Mass,* especially in the first chapter, Scripture passages are frequently quoted in the essays. You may wish to skip over these passages during your first reading of the chapter and then return to them for a second, more reflective reading of the entire chapter. This would be an ideal way to study first the particular origins of the rite and then prepare for a week of meditation through a slower and more reflective reading, with the focus on the Scriptures themselves.

During the week of meditations provided at the end of each chapter, you are encouraged to spend at least five to fifteen minutes in daily meditation. For this time of reflection read the text of the meditation and Scripture a couple of times slowly and reflectively. Then select a particular verse or phrase for the focus of your meditation. Consider keeping a prayer journal, so you can jot down any thoughts or reflections that come to you in daily meditation.

In organizing groups for weekly discussion, you may be able to review the material with prayer groups, parish renewal groups, through religious education programs in your parish—or even form an impromptu neighborhood group composed of Catholic friends and acquaintances. Such groups will need to consider set starting and closing times for group meetings, a format for the group's time together, and an approach to group leadership. Keep in mind that you may want to take two weeks to cover the material in chapter three on the Liturgy of the Eucharist since it is a long chapter. If so, a logical approach would be to study the four Eucharistic Prayers during your second week of study on the chapter.

Besides chapters on the various rites of the Mass, this

book includes three appendices. The first appendix explains the place of Latin in the Church's liturgy, seeking to dispel many misconceptions about its valid use in the liturgy today. The last two appendices provide helpful background information on posture in worship, sacred vestments, liturgical colors, and other objects used in the liturgy. Study questions are included after the appendices, so you can study the material and then meet for another time of group discussion.

One final note: in using this book, you will need a Sunday Missal for the complete text of the rites of the liturgy—including the four Eucharistic Prayers. If possible, a copy of the *New American Bible* would also be helpful for reference: the 1986 edition with the revised New Testament. This is the translation of Scripture used in the liturgy and in this book.

May your understanding of the liturgy increase and your participation in the Mass grow as you read, reflect, and meditate on the connection between the Bible and the Mass.

Introduction:
The Sacred Mysteries

"MY BROTHERS AND SISTERS, to prepare ourselves to celebrate the sacred mysteries..." Thus, the celebrant opens the Penitential Rite of the Mass. But what does the Church mean here by "the sacred mysteries"?

The word "mystery" carries many connotations. The dictionary tells us a mystery can be: A secret, something hidden or unknown; a person or situation which has unexplained elements, such that curiosity and speculation are aroused; secrecy and obscurity; something not explained or understood; a religious doctrine which unaided human reason cannot fully appreciate; a secret religious rite to which only the fully initiated are admitted.

In varying degrees, the Church intends all these meanings to be apprehended as she speaks of "the sacred mysteries." This becomes even clearer when one realizes that the Greek *mysterion* was translated into Latin by *sacramentum*; mystery and sacrament are then two sides of the same coin as what is hidden is revealed. What happens in the Mass is that God's mysterious plan, conceived from all eternity and brought to its fulfillment in His divine Son's passion, death, and resurrection, is made present. Or, as Pope St. Leo the Great put it, "What our Redeemer did visibly has passed over into the sacraments."

Our present recollection of a past event occurs through the use of special signs and symbols. For the liturgy to be able to accomplish its work to the full, those signs and symbols particular to it must be understood. All too often people complain that they "get nothing out of the Mass." I am persuaded that with nearly as great a frequency they fail to comprehend the significance of the rites. Therefore, they do not know what to expect and thus apparently receive nothing.

The holy Sacrifice of the Mass, however, is a marvelous drama—jointly produced by Christ and His Church. Just as the Holy Spirit inspired the sacred authors of the Scriptures to communicate the Word of God in the words of men, so too did that same Holy Spirit lead the Church to take the central redeeming acts of our blessed Savior and to surround them with signs and symbols.

In this way, the offer of salvation would be continuously renewed until He comes again in glory, bringing His faithful people into the liturgy of heaven. On that day, all the veils will be removed; signs and symbols— the sacraments—shall cease because they will have served their purpose in leading us from the darkness into the light, indeed to the Light.

Until that moment, however, we walk by faith, not by sight. Like Moses of old, we behold the *mysterium tremendum et fascinans;* we are in awe yet curious. It is a holy awe and a holy curiosity. With Moses, we take off our shoes, for we are on holy ground. Likewise, with Moses, we approach the burning bush to plumb the mystery (Ex 3), confident that we shall not be harmed but rather warmed and enlightened.

In this process, we too shall learn anew God's Name: I Am Who Am—the Source of Existence—Life Itself. That life is communicated to His Son's Church through "the sacred mysteries."

CHAPTER ONE

COMING INTO HIS PRESENCE: INTRODUCTORY RITES

Coming into His Presence: Introductory Rites

"**H**OW DO I BEGIN TO TELL the great love story that is older than the sea?" The song-writer was not the first to raise that question. It may well have been the thought in the minds of the individuals who gave form and shape to the earliest liturgies in the Church. The mystery we celebrate is so great and so much a story of God's love for His people, that it is indeed difficult to know just where and how to begin, but begin we must.

In the Eucharistic Sacrifice we celebrate not only the sacramental representation of the Savior's once-for-all salvation wrought on Calvary (Heb 10:10), but also the symbolic marriage of God and His people, Christ and His Church. We are the bride of Christ, adorned and ready for the bridegroom:

"Come here. I will show you the bride, the wife of the Lamb." He took me in spirit to a great, high mountain and showed me the holy city Jerusalem coming down out of heaven from God. It gleamed with the splendor of God. Its radiance was like that of a precious stone, like jasper, clear as crystal.

(Rv 21:9b-11)

Therefore, one can say that the liturgy begins when the people, precisely as the members of Christ's body, gather to hear God's Word and to celebrate His work of self-giving.

ENTRANCE SONG

An opening hymn accompanies the procession of the priest and the other ministers of the Mass. This hymn or entrance antiphon (usually a verse or two of a psalm) helps to establish the mood for the particular day's celebration. It gives musical expression to the psalmist's determination to go in procession to the house of God amid cries of gladness and joy:

Send forth your light and your fidelity;
     they shall lead me on
And bring me to your holy mountain,
     to your dwelling-place.
Then will I go in to the altar of God,
     the God of my gladness and joy;
Then will I give you thanks upon the harp,
     O God, my God! (Ps 43:3-4)

Ideally, this prayer should be sung; in fact, as much

as possible should be sung during the sacred liturgy, not merely to add greater solemnity but because of the truth of St. Augustine's insight that one who "sings well prays twice." The procession is not just a means used to arrive in the sanctuary; it has deep theological significance, reminding all of the fact that the entire people of God is a pilgrim people *in via,* on the road from here to eternity. In that sacred journey Christ is not only our final goal (symbolized by the altar), but He accompanies us on the way (in the person of the priest).

As the procession reaches the altar, priest and ministers genuflect to the Blessed Sacrament, if it is visible from the central axis, or else bow profoundly to the altar. The priest kisses the altar, in effect, greeting Christ. In all likelihood, this gesture has its origins in the fact that the Eucharistic Sacrifice was first offered in the catacombs on the tombs of the martyrs—those valiant believers who continued the passion and death of the Lord in their own lives. When the Church was able to come above ground after centuries of persecution, she took this custom with her by inserting a stone into the altar, with the relics of martyrs enclosed, thus maintaining the link between the paschal mystery of Christ, its continuation in the saints, and its reenactment in the Mass.

Interestingly, the altar stone also came to signify Christ as the cornerstone of that building which is the Church, His body:

Come to him, a living stone, rejected by human beings but chosen and precious in the sight of God, and, like living stones, let yourselves be built into a spiritual house to be a holy priesthood to offer spiritual sacrifices acceptable to God through Jesus Christ. For it says in Scripture:

"Behold, I am laying a stone in Zion,
    a cornerstone, chosen and precious,
and whoever believes in it shall not be put to
    shame."(1 Pt 2:4-6)

GREETING

Having reverenced the altar, the priest and people then trace the sign of the cross over themselves, that sign by which we were saved at Baptism:

"Go, therefore, and make disciples of all nations, baptizing them in the name of the Father, and of the Son, and of the holy Spirit, teaching them to observe all that I have commanded you. And behold, I am with you always, until the end of the age."
(Mt 28:19-20)

The priest then wishes for the people the grace and peace of God, which he has received from his kissing of the altar, so that one can say that it is truly the Lord who greets His community of faithful people. That is why secular greetings, like "Good morning," are so out of place. What is offered to the congregation here is more than a simple courtesy. It is nothing less than a prayer for the salvation of all present.

On solemn occasions the sign of the cross and greetings are preceded by the incensing of the altar, which is both an act of reverence and purification. The smoke rises to heaven and serves as a sign of our own desire to have our prayers ascend heavenward in God's sight:

> O LORD, to you I call; hasten to me;
>   hearken to my voice when I call upon you.
> Let my prayer come like incense before you;
>   the lifting up of my hands, like the evening
>   sacrifice. (Ps 141:1-2)

At this point in the liturgy, the incensing is most especially done to prepare the site of worship. Later on at the Offertory, it will have much more the meaning of veneration for sacred persons and objects.

PENITENTIAL RITE

The work of preparation proceeds as the celebrant invites the congregation to examine their consciences, in order to enter into these sacred mysteries in as worthy a manner as possible. We know that no human being is ever fully worthy to approach the all-holy God, but that does not diminish the need to remove as many obstacles as possible. And so, we reflect not only on our sinful state as children of Adam and Eve but specifically on our own complicity in that sinfulness through personal acts that have offended Almighty God:

> For I acknowledge my offense,
>   and my sin is before me always:
> "Against you only have I sinned,
>   and done what is evil in your sight"—
> That you may be justified in your sentence,
>   vindicated when you condemn. (Ps 51:5-6)

If the first form of the Penitential Rite is used, the alienation effected by sin is powerfully portrayed in the use of the first person singular pronoun. It is the only time in the liturgy when a worshiper speaks as an "I" rather than as part of a "we." And how appropriate that is, for sin does build barriers between the individual and God, between the individual and others in the community of the redeemed, and even within the individual himself.

The *Confiteor*, however, does more than note the disoriented desire for autonomy in a sinner; it goes on to offer a remedy in the appeal to the communion of saints, which is the Church. Having acknowledged both "what I have done" and "what I have failed to do," the repentant sinner seeks comfort and help in Christian solidarity by beseeching the intercession of the Blessed Virgin Mary, Mother of Christ and Mother of the Church, and that of all the saints and angels (who, we should remember, were also subject to a time of testing):

> Blessed are they who wash their robes so as to have the right to the tree of life and enter the city through its gates. Outside are the dogs, the sorcerers, the unchaste, the murderers, the idol-worshipers, and all who love and practice deceit.
>
> (Rv 22:14-15)

From that moment forward, one is entitled to act and speak as part of the "we," which is Christ's sinless bride.

The confession of sin would be either a self-defeating or depressing exercise were it not followed by the declaration of forgiveness in the prayer of absolution. God's loving forgiveness is greater than our human sinfulness. It should be noted, however, that this formula of absolution does not free one from grievous sin, which requires a personal sacramental encounter with Christ through the agency of the priest. Mortal sin might well be repented of then, with the firm resolution to confess such sins at the earliest opportunity, but neither the resolution nor the prayer at that moment entitle one to reenter the fullness of the communion of saints by partaking of eucharistic communion in that celebration.

KYRIE

The prayer for mercy common to the Churches of East and West is the *Kyrie, Eleison* ("Lord, have mercy"), echoing the sentiments of sinners from biblical times to our very own, like David who cries out in Psalm 51: "Have mercy on me, O God, in your goodness" (v.1). It is interesting that even when the liturgy of the Western Church began to use Latin, this prayer was maintained in the original Greek as a way of demonstrating the antiquity of the prayer and as a means of expressing the fundamental unity between the two great branches of the Church. In the revised liturgy of the Roman Rite, the *Kyrie* is still recited in Greek. Some truly marvelous and moving musical settings exist for this prayer of humility and hope.

GLORIA

On Sundays (except during Advent and Lent because of their penitential character) and on major feasts, the *Gloria* is now prayed—the first lines of which hymn St. Luke's Gospel tells us were sung by the angels to herald our Savior's birth:

> And suddenly there was a multitude of the heavenly host with the angel, praising God and saying:

> "Glory to God in the highest
> and on earth peace to those on whom
> his favor rests." (Lk 2:13-14)

How right it is to intone these same words as we prepare to receive Him here on earth once again, this time under sacramental signs, but in a presence every bit as real as what Mary and Joseph and the shepherds beheld that first Christmas night.

OPENING PRAYER

The Introductory Rites conclude with the Opening Prayer, known as the *Collect* in Latin, because it is a collection or culmination of the petitions of the congregation for that particular celebration. The *Collect*, like the entrance antiphon, helps to set the tone for the Mass of the day. It is important to stress that our prayers in the liturgy are always made to the Father, through the Son, in the power of the Holy Spirit. This will be clearest in the offering of the Eucharistic Prayer, but it is certainly true of the Opening Prayer, the Prayer over the Gifts, and the Prayer after Communion as well. This prayer to the Father gives acknowledgment to the fact that our prayer, whether as individuals or even as Christ's Church, has value only to the extent that it is united to Christ's own prayer to His heavenly Father, done preeminently in His self-offering on the cross.

One can see that the several prayers of the Mass to this point form a unity, leading us in a kind of crescendo, whereby we are brought from a sinful world into the presence of God and made worthy to approach Him, so as to hear His Word and to participate in the offering of the Eucharistic Sacrifice and in the reception of the fruits of that sacrifice.

SCRIPTURAL MEDITATIONS FOR THE INTRODUCTORY RITES

1. In the name of the Father, and of the Son, and of the Holy Spirit: (The Greeting) (Mt 28:19, text is the same)

As we begin our celebration of the sacred mysteries, we do so in the Name of the Blessed Trinity, in Whose Name we were first incorporated into Christ through Baptism, and in Whose Name Christians perform every action. The Eucharist is offered as an act of praise and thanksgiving to the Triune God—to the Father Who created us; to the Son Who redeemed us precisely in and through the paschal mysteries herein recalled; to the Holy Spirit Who sanctifies us, most especially through the Church's sacraments.

In reciting the ancient words, we trace over our bodies the sign of the cross. A legend notes that the Emperor Constantine was launched on the road to his conversion with a vision of the cross and the words: *In hoc signo vinces* ("In this sign you shall conquer"). In truth, it is through Christ's cross that we have conquered the mortal enemies of humanity since the Garden of Eden—the world, the flesh, and the Devil. Indeed, it was from the Lord's wounded side, as He hung upon the cross, that blood and water flowed out—symbols of Baptism and the Eucharist:

> But when they came to Jesus and saw that he was already dead, they did not break his legs, but one soldier thrust his lance into his side, and immediately blood and water flowed out. An eyewitness has testified, and his testimony is true; he knows that he is speaking the truth, so that you also may [come to] believe. (Jn 19:33-35)

In each Mass, the baptismal formula and the cross are joined at the very outset as the grace of our Baptism is renewed and increased through the celebration of the Eucharist.

May what has been begun in the Name of the Blessed Trinity, under sacramental signs, lead us to the unveiled vision of the Triune God for all eternity.

2. The grace of our Lord Jesus Christ and the love of God and the fellowship of the Holy Spirit be with you all. (The Greeting) (2 Cor 13:13, text is nearly identical to the Greeting)

Grace is God's completely free and unmerited favor toward us. Grace is the gift of God encompassing all other gifts. Through grace God communicates His own life to broken humanity. We become like God Himself. This transformation by grace has its source and power in the incarnation of our blessed Lord.

The love of God is open-ended and sacrificial, most clearly revealed in the gift of His divine Son. As the fourth Gospel puts it so succinctly and powerfully: "God so loved the world that he gave his only Son, so that everyone who believes in him might not perish but might have eternal life" (Jn 3:16).

What of the fellowship of the Holy Spirit? This is a relationship having vertical and horizontal dimensions. First, it refers to the communion which exists between the believer and the Blessed Trinity. Second, it is concerned with the way in which the members of the Church relate to one another—as brothers and sisters in Christ. Both forms of communion are the work of the Holy Spirit, and both aspects of Christian fellowship are fostered and increased through the Eucharist: "Whoever eats my flesh and drinks my blood remains in me and I in him" (Jn 6:56).

In effect, when the priest greets the community assembled for worship with this prayer, he wishes for each of them the very realities which each person of the Trinity manifests to the Church: The Father's selfless love; the Son's gracious act of self-donation; the Holy Spirit's sanctifying and unifying work of grace, whereby Christians are joined to God and one another more intimately and completely.

Indeed, we pray for profound gifts as the Eucharistic Sacrifice begins. However, because the sacrifice is that of Christ, it is not presumptuous to seek such favors. Our faith instructs us that, if we cooperate with the divine promptings offered in the liturgy, we have every right to expect nothing less than these marvelous means of deepening the divine life first bestowed on us in Baptism.

3. **The Lord be with you.** (The Greeting)

Boaz himself came from Bethlehem and said to the harvesters, "The LORD be with you!" and they replied, "The LORD bless you!" (Ru 2:4)

We hear this greeting several times at Mass, and we have heard it so often that it has lost its startling character. Many have grown tired of hearing it. They no longer view it as a revelatory greeting but only as one more response to be given. This is most unfortunate.

The next time you participate in the Mass, listen for those words and try to experience them for the first time—in all their dazzling audacity. The priest is praying that the Lord will come and make His dwelling within you. He is asking Almighty God to come to everyone in the assembly and to make each one a faithful reflection of the God Who lives within each baptized and sanctified believer. He is beseeching the Christ of the sacraments to come into our hearts, to maintain and strengthen His gift of grace.

By your response, *And also with you* (The Greeting), you assert that you are aware of this tremendous wish, indicating that you desire the same for the celebrant. This heartfelt wish unites the entire Christian family in a common desire. Actually, it is the most basic Christian prayer possible, for if the Lord is not with us, we cannot be Christians. With the Lord, we can perform great works because of His power and life within us. Without Him, we can do nothing.

4. May almighty God have mercy on us, forgive us our sins, and bring us to everlasting life. Amen. (The Penitential Rite, the Prayer of Absolution)

"Let us pray and beg our Lord to have mercy on us and to grant us deliverance." (Tb 8:4b)

Christianity is the most consoling religion in the history of humanity's attempts to enter into a relationship with God. However, God's mercy to us in Christ rules out passivity and complacency as a response. Instead, we are urged on to do greater and better things for the glory of Christ and His Church.

Other gods made harsh demands on their people, even to demanding the sacrifice of children. But the God of the Hebrews, Whom Jesus revealed to us as *Abba* (an affectionate and intimate term for "father") offered salvation and comfort to His children:

As proof that you are children, God sent the spirit of his Son into our hearts, crying out, "Abba, Father!" So you are no longer a slave but a child, and if a child then also an heir, through God. (Gal 4:6-7)

In the same way, our divine Savior tells His disciples: "I no longer call you slaves, because a slave does not know what his master is doing. I have called you friends . . ." (Jn 15:15).

Yes, we know what Jesus is about; His work was— and still is—to save the human family by bringing us back to God. It is in the person of Christ that the priest absolves us of our sins in the Penitential Rite. This saving work is continued through the mission and sacramental life of the Church.

In the Introductory Rites, the comforting news of God's love and nearness to all is proclaimed. Here we are presented with the message of reconciliation after entering God's presence:

> And all this is from God, who has reconciled us to himself through Christ and given us the ministry of reconciliation, namely, God was reconciling the world to himself in Christ, not counting their trespasses against them and entrusting to us the message of reconciliation. So we are ambassadors for Christ, as if God were appealing through us. We implore you on behalf of Christ, be reconciled to God. For our sake he made him to be sin who did not know sin, so that we might become the righteousness of God in him. (2 Cor 5:18-21)

This is the God Who came not to condemn but to save: "For God did not send his Son into the world to condemn the world, but that the world might be saved through him" (Jn 3:17).

5. **Glory to God in the highest and peace to his people on earth.** (The Gloria)

> *Now there were shepherds in that region living in the fields and keeping the night watch over their flock. The angel of the Lord appeared to them and the glory of the Lord shone*

around them, and they were struck with great fear. The angel said to them, "Do not be afraid; for behold, I proclaim to you good news of great joy that will be for all the people. For today in the city of David a savior has been born for you who is Messiah and Lord. And this will be a sign for you: you will find an infant wrapped in swaddling clothes and lying in a manger." And suddenly there was a multitude of the heavenly host with the angel, praising God and saying:

*"Glory to God in the highest
and on earth peace to those on whom his favor rests."*
(Lk 2:8-14)

Glory in English, *doxa* in Greek, *kabod* in Hebrew. It means praise, honor, majesty, power, holiness. In any language, it is the duty and privilege of every man and woman to recognize the glory of God. Yet we know that many human beings, if not most of us, fail to acknowledge that glory because of sin, which veils God's glory. Reflect on these passages, for example:

But now, what am I to do here?
  says the LORD.
My people have been taken away without redress;
  their rulers make a boast of it, says the LORD;
  all the day my name is constantly reviled. (Is 52:5)

But when they came among the nations [wherever they came], they served to profane my holy name, because it was said of them: "These are the people of the LORD, yet they had to leave their land." (Ez 36:20)

For, as it is written, "Because of you the name of God is reviled among the Gentiles." (Rom 2:24)

This doxology or hymn of praise is central to the offering of the Eucharistic Sacrifice, for even when it is not used, its sentiments express what is essential to a worthy offering. If the doxology is not to be meaninglessly repeated every Sunday, it must be supported by the witness of a holy life, in which the Church plays a unique role, just as she does in the celebration of the Eucharist itself: "... to him be glory in the church and in Christ Jesus to all generations, forever and ever. Amen" (Eph 3:21).

Indeed, through her preaching of the Word and through her celebration of the sacraments, the Church gives to her sons and daughters the means to render to God the glory due His holy Name. When that happens, then sin is routed. Only then can the next line of the Gloria take root as peace—God's peace—becomes a reality in the lives of "his people on earth."

Recognizing the glory of God—in word and in deed—is the only true way to the longed-for experiences of true and lasting peace. It is a peace that only Christ and His Church can give.

6. Lord Jesus Christ, only Son of the Father, Lord God, Lamb of God, . . . (The Gloria)

Because of this, God greatly exalted him
and bestowed on him the name
that is above every name,

> *that at the name of Jesus*
> *every knee should bend,*
> *of those in heaven and on earth and under the earth,*
> *and every tongue confess that*
> *Jesus Christ is Lord,*
> *to the glory of God the Father.* (Phil 2:9-11)

In the Gloria, we address Jesus as the only Son of the Father, as the One Who alone is holy, the Lord and the Most High. These are clear references to Jesus' role in salvation and His divinity as the Lord God.

The birth of our Lord split history in two. *Never has a man been honored like Jesus.* He has been the inspiration for the writing of countless books. Great symphonies and oratorios have been composed in His honor. Sermons have been preached on His message of salvation for nearly two millennia. Saints and martyrs of the church have lived and died for Him. Truly did Isaiah prophesy of Him:

> For a child is born to us, a son is given us;
> upon his shoulder dominion rests.
> They name him Wonder-Counselor, God-Hero,
> Father-Forever, Prince of Peace.
> His dominion is vast
> and forever peaceful,
> From David's throne, and over his kingdom,
> which he confirms and sustains
> By judgment and justice,
> both now and forever.
> The zeal of the LORD of hosts will do this! (Is 9:5-6)

What is the strong magnetism of Jesus? The simplicity of His birth, His obedience in childhood, His faithfulness and dedication in public ministry, the sacrifice of His own life, His return to life, and the continuation of His life and mission through His Church.

With St. Paul, we must humbly bow before this great mystery and simply confess that Jesus Christ is Lord: Lord of history, Lord of the Church, Lord of our lives.

7. **Amen**. (The Great Acclamation)

> *Blessed be the LORD, the God of Israel,*
>   *through all eternity!*
> *Let all the people say, Amen! Alleluia.* (1 Chr 16:36)

Dozens of times during the Mass, the congregation says "Amen." What is its significance?

Literally, it can be translated as "So be it," "So it is," or "Yes, indeed." This response expresses not only agreement with the prayer which has just been said, but also declares our commitment to a particular proposition and proclaims our sense of responsibility to follow through by taking the appropriate course of action, whatever it might be. This response is especially linked to our collective commitment to God as His people, expressed at different points in the sacred liturgy.

Reflect on these Scriptures:

I also shook out the folds of my garment, saying, "Thus may God shake from his home and his fortune every man who fails to keep this promise, and may he thus be shaken out and emptied!" And the whole assembly answered, "Amen," and praised the LORD. Then the people did as they had promised.

(Neh 5:13)

At the same time, we realize that God has said a firm, definitive "Amen" to us in Christ: "For however many are the promises of God, their Yes is in him; therefore, the Amen from us also goes through him to God for glory" (2 Cor 1:20).

Therefore, we are motivated to respond "Amen" in return:

"Amen. Blessing and glory, wisdom and thanks-
    giving,
honor, power, and might
be to our God forever and ever. Amen." (Rv 7:12)

How does this occur? Only under the impulse of divine grace, which is first imparted to us in our Baptism: "The grace of the Lord Jesus be with all" (Rv 22:21). That impulse is strengthened in each celebration of the Mass as we grow in the ability to do, with God's help, what our weakened human nature would find otherwise very difficult, if not impossible.

Most simply put, God's "Amen" to us in Christ makes possible and necessary our own "Amen" to God, as His people and as individuals.

Questions for Group Discussion

1. Why does the celebrant reverence the altar at the beginning of the liturgy? What exactly does the celebrant do?

2. Why are secular greetings inappropriate for the Greeting during the Introductory Rites?

Note: Throughout this book, space has been provided after questions for group discussion so you can write down your answers before meeting with your group.

3. To whom is the *Kyrie* (Lord, have mercy) addressed? Why is an exception made here? Discuss.

4. Explain the dramatic structure of the Introductory Rites. What is the climax? Why?

5. What is the main purpose of the Introductory Rites? Discuss.

GOD SPEAKS TO US: THE LITURGY OF THE WORD

God Speaks to Us: The Liturgy of the Word

WITH MINDS AND HEARTS purified and renewed, the people of God now listen to God's Word. But in order to appreciate more fully the proclamation and preaching of the Word of God, we need to delve into the historical roots of the Liturgy of the Word.

First, it is helpful to note that prior to the liturgical revisions following the Second Vatican Council, this part of the liturgy was called the Mass of the Catechumens because of its highly instructional nature. This meant that those preparing for Baptism (the catechumens) would only attend this portion of the liturgy. After the Creed, the catechumens were dismissed, and the Mass of the Faithful (now termed the Liturgy of the Eucharist) began.

Second, the Liturgy of the Word has its origins in Jewish Tradition, patterned after the example of Jesus and the first Christians, who were devout Jews. We know from the Scriptures that Jesus prayed daily in private; He faithfully attended His local synagogue; and He participated in the Temple liturgies in Jerusalem.

His early followers imitated His example, so that the first Church history textbook tells us: "Every day they devoted themselves to meeting together in the temple area and to breaking bread in their homes" (Acts 2:46). In other words, those early believers in Christ held on to their Jewish traditions and then added to them the specifically Christian "breaking of the bread" of the Eucharist.

In time, the Jewish authorities in Jerusalem, beleaguered from without by the Romans, came to the conclusion that the presence of these "Nazarenes" within their community was divisive and had to be eliminated. Hence, a benediction (really a malediction) found its way into the synagogue liturgy, cursing the "sectarians" and effectively driving them out of institutional Judaism.

Upon leaving Judaism, these early Christians took the synagogue service and combined it with the breaking of the bread—replete with passover symbols like Jesus as the Lamb of God. Thus, the Mass throughout the ages has been a service in two parts: Liturgy of the Word and Liturgy of the Eucharist.

In drawing upon Judaism, these first liturgists looked primarily to the party of the Pharisees who had founded the synagogues, which were focused on prayer and Scripture reading in the local Jewish community. Early Christianity incorporated not only basic

Pharisaic doctrines (like the resurrection of the dead) but also Pharisaic prayer forms, reflecting Christ's own predisposition to Pharisaism, even if He often disagreed with the Pharisees' style or methods of operation.

Synagogue worship, right up to the present, is a heavily verbal ritual, including prayers, psalms, and Scripture readings. It also includes the primitive Jewish creed: "Hear, O Israel, the Lord our God is Lord alone . . . ," and various blessings or benedictions.

The Scripture readings in our Lord's time were based on a three-year cycle, just as they are in the present Catholic liturgy. The Hebrew lectionary began on the Sabbath after the Feast of Tabernacles and ended on the last day of the same feast. It provided for a continuous reading from the Torah (the first five books of the Bible) and also a passage from one of the prophets, used to explain the first reading or the particular feast. This is precisely the notion behind our selection of readings: The Second Reading is generally continuous from one of the epistles, while the Gospel and First Reading from the Hebrew Scriptures dovetail.

In synagogue worship, the Torah was carried to the *bima* (lectern or pulpit) in solemn procession, accompanied by the singing of psalms. The appropriate readings were then chanted by a priest, levite, or scholar (in order of preference), especially if this occurred in the synagogue attached to the Temple. The congregation responded to the readings with the equivalent of our "Thanks be to God," and the sacred scroll was returned to the ark, which was a model of the Ark of the Covenant.

THE CYCLE OF READINGS

In our own worship service the biblical readings are taken from the lectionary—a liturgical book which sets forth the required readings for each day of the year and for special rites. The Sunday lectionary is a three-year cycle of three readings. The First Reading usually comes from the Old Testament and parallels the Gospel passage in theme, showing how the Hebrew Bible prepared for the definitive revelation of the Gospel in Christ. The Second Reading is generally taken from one of the epistles or the Book of Revelation.

The Gospel pericopes or readings are arranged in such a way that in the season throughout the year (Ordinary Time, the "green" season)—Cycle A relies on the Gospel according to St. Matthew; Cycle B, on Mark; Cycle C, on Luke. St. John's Gospel is used in all three cycles and especially during the Sundays in Lent during Cycle A. The weekday readings are presented on a two-year cycle. Specific attention is given to passages not covered on Sundays.

If a Catholic were to read no Scripture beyond the texts used for Sunday Mass over the three-year period, that person would have been exposed to more than seven thousand verses of the Bible—no mean accomplishment. Of course, Bible reading has always formed the first half of the Mass from apostolic times (as the New Testament itself attests), but the lectionary revised since the Second Vatican Council opened up even more of the Bible to the Sunday-Mass Catholic.

The new lectionary is so extensive in its coverage of nearly the entire New Testament and the most significant portions of the Old Testament over the three years that most main-line Protestant denominations have adopted it as well. In fact, if a Catholic attends daily Mass, the percentage of Scripture proclaimed over a two-year span is more than double that of the Sunday figure.

Unfortunately, Catholics have often been under the misperception that Protestants read more of the Bible than Catholics, but that is not necessarily true—either quantitatively or qualitatively, but especially qualitatively. Many Protestant preachers and ministers select biblical passages according to the topic they wish to handle for a given day. Thus, it is not unusual for them to have favorite themes and key passages to which their congregations are treated on a recurring basis.

Fortunately, this kind of eclectic or selective Bible reading is not possible in the Catholic liturgy because the readings are assigned to a particular day. Hence, the homily must flow from the Word of God; the cleric's pet themes or interests do not determine the sections of the Word of God to be proclaimed. This is not an insignificant point to understand and appreciate.

The biblical texts are especially relevant as the Church seeks to unfold the mystery of Christ during the course of the special seasons of the liturgical year. In Advent, therefore, our gaze is directed toward the Messiah's coming, with the prophet Isaiah as a most appropriate guide. In Lent, the scriptural readings are devoted to a consideration of sin, repentance, and reconciliation. At Christmas and Easter, the memorable passages related to these important feasts are proclaimed in the liturgical assembly.

THE RITE OF THE LITURGY OF THE WORD

With this historical background and understanding of the present-day Liturgy of the Word, let us now consider the order of the rite itself. First, it is important to keep in mind that the proclamation of the Word is focused on two time periods: The readings present the activity of Almighty God in history, while the homily and the Profession of Faith deal with the present-day application and acceptance of the Word.

The lay reader (male or female) or officially installed lector (male) goes to the lectern or pulpit and reads the first lesson as the people sit and listen attentively. That is followed by the responsorial psalm, recited (or better, sung) in alternation between the reader (or cantor) and the congregation. This psalm is intended to be a meditative response to the message of the First Reading. On Sundays, a second reading is offered.

After a suitable period of silent reflection, the cantor

intones the Alleluia, a joyful cry of praise to God. It is so connected to an attitude of rejoicing that it is replaced during Lent by another form of Gospel acclamation. In fact, an interesting monastic tradition calls for a scroll with the Alleluia verse written on it to be buried in the monastery graveyard after it is sung on the Sunday before Lent. It is then "resurrected" and sung for the first time at the Easter Vigil Liturgy over six weeks later.

The Gospel is treated with singular reverence since in and through it, Christ speaks in a unique way to His people. Only a sacred minister in Holy Orders reads or chants the Gospel. The sacred text is incensed on solemn occasions, as the reader is flanked by two acolytes with lighted candles, representing Christ the Light. If a deacon is the reader of the Gospel, he seeks the celebrant's blessing; if a priest or bishop, he prepares himself by a prayer asking God to "cleanse my heart and my lips that I may worthily proclaim your gospel."

The congregation stands out of respect and are greeted by the sacred minister, who announces the passage to be read. Simultaneously, all make the Sign of the cross on the forehead, lips, and heart, signifying the desire to open their minds and hearts to the Gospel message and to ready their lips to share that message with others. The Book of the Gospels is kissed, just like the altar, since both are points of contact with the living Christ.

After the Gospel, a homily is preached by a bishop, priest, or deacon, usually by the celebrant of the Mass.

The Church considers this preaching so valuable that it is required on Sundays and holy days of obligation. It is strongly recommended even for weekdays, especially during Lent and Advent. Unlike a sermon (which could be a discourse on any religious topic), a homily draws its inspiration principally from the biblical readings of the day's liturgy or from some aspect of the eucharistic mystery being celebrated.

The Church insists that the homilist be an ordained minister not simply because of the theological training necessary to preach (after all, there are many speakers among the religious and laity in parishes today who are better educated and more eloquent than some priests). Rather, as Catholics we are convinced that the Sacrament of Holy Orders confers a unique charism and grace which empowers a man to speak for God in a supernatural manner. In fact, when the priest-celebrant is the homilist, a wonderful connection is maintained as the same man is the instrument for making Christ present in both Word and Sacrament.

THE PROFESSION OF FAITH

After a time of meditation, all rise to recite the Nicene Creed on Sundays and major feasts (the Apostles' Creed may be substituted in Masses for children). The Creed was inserted into the liturgy as a means of ensuring that only true believers would remain for the Liturgy of the Eucharist. In this regard, it is fascinating to note that the Creed was absent from the liturgical celebration in Rome until as late as the eleventh century. The reason is that the See of Rome—as guardian of the true faith—was never plagued by heresy. Hence, there was no perceived need for a profession of faith.

In our modern context, the Creed represents the assent of the entire congregation to the Word of God which has been read and preached. As such, it is a communal act, underscored by the use of the pronoun "we." Although the Latin *credo* means "I believe," its Greek forerunner declared that "we believe" (*pisteuomen*). Of course, the communal action means nothing if the personal commitment is lacking.

The Creed is also known as the symbol of faith. In Greek, *symbolon* comes from the verb *symballein*, meaning "to throw together," as in to synthesize. The Creed makes a unity of the Christian faith and of all people who profess it. *Diaballein*, on the other hand, means "to throw into confusion," the source of our English word "diabolical." Sureness of faith in authentic teaching and in faithful acceptance effects unity. Thus, confusion in these areas is truly diabolical—the work of the devil to disrupt the unity of Christ's Church.

At the words which recall the incarnation, all bow (genuflect on the feasts of the Annunciation and Christmas, March 25 and December 25). Since we worship as embodied beings, our physical gestures are important signs of our interior disposition of the heart.

In this instance, we give acknowledgment to the most momentous event in human history—an event soon to be sacramentalized in the Liturgy of the Eucharist.

GENERAL INTERCESSIONS

Before entering upon the second major part of the Mass, the Church intercedes for herself and all humanity. These petitions are placed before Almighty God as intentions for which the Eucharistic Sacrifice is offered. These General Intercessions or Prayer of the Faithful was reintroduced into the Roman liturgy after Vatican II. Prior to the Council, the most ancient liturgy of the Roman Rite still in use was the Good Friday service, in which an extended Prayer of the Faithful is most prominent. These petitions follow a certain standardized formula and order: the celebrant begins the prayer; a lector, deacon, or cantor reads (or sings) the specific intentions; the people respond by asking the Lord to hear our prayer; the celebrant sums up all our intercessions in a concluding prayer.

The General Intercessions should deal with matters of concern to the Church (her unity and leaders, evangelization, and vocations), the world (justice and peace, God's guidance of civil officials), and the needs of the local Christian community (the sick and the faithful departed).

The dramatic action has now reached the first plateau, and the liturgical assembly is prepared to move on to the next level, where the Word will become flesh.

SCRIPTURAL MEDITATIONS FOR
THE LITURGY OF THE WORD

1. This is the Word of the Lord. (Liturgy of the Word)

Then he said to me: Prophesy over these bones, and say to them: Dry bones, hear the word of the LORD! (Ez 37:4)

Imagine a field of skeletons coming to life, and all because they heard the Word of the Lord! Yes, God's Word can do marvelous things but, as St. Paul reminds us, that Word needs a preacher (Rom 10:17). Through Baptism every believer is commissioned to be a preacher of the Gospel. In the course of the liturgy of the sacrament, the priest says to the newly baptized: "The Lord Jesus made the deaf hear and the dumb speak. May He soon touch your ears to receive His Word and your mouth to proclaim His faith, to the praise and glory of God the Father."

Dry bones lie all around us; they need to be quickened by God's Word. It is our obligation and our privilege to be God's spokespersons. To be effective, this preaching must be done not only with our lips but with our lives. Then will the amazing vision of Ezekiel become a reality in our own day.

2. The Lord be in your heart and on your lips that you may worthily proclaim his gospel. (Liturgy of the Word)

Son of man, eat what is before you; eat this scroll, then go, speak to the house of Israel. (Ez 3:1)

The Germans have a proverb which says: "A man is what he eats." Is this what God had in mind when he told Ezekiel to eat the scroll? In consuming something, that thing becomes a part of us. When we "take in" the Scriptures, we cannot help but be affected by their message, and God expects us to pass on that message to others.

Actually, that is what we are about in this part of the Mass. We are consuming parts of Scripture in the hope that the newfound knowledge will cause a change in us. How does this process occur?

We accomplish this by careful reading and rereading, by prayerful reflection on the passages, by applying them to our own daily lives, and by deciding how to put these thoughts and applications into action. If these elements are not included in our reading of sacred Scripture, we run the risk of making this a mere academic exercise. Undoubtedly, we will gain knowledge, but our primary purpose should be to effect a change in our lifestyle—to make one a better, stronger believer.

Take the lessons of Scripture to heart. Learn from every biblical character, even the character lessons to be drawn from the bad ones. With the good models Scripture provides, resolve to emulate their virtues. With the bad, resolve never to go the way they went.

Like the Church, the Scriptures are a gift to us from God. Our faith tells us that the religious message of the Scriptures, composed under the guidance of the Holy Spirit, will never fail us. The same Holy Spirit who inspired the sacred authors to write will also inspire us to put their writings into action.

"Indeed, the word of God is living and effective, sharper than any two-edged sword, penetrating even between soul and spirit, joints and marrow, and able to discern reflections and thoughts of the heart" (Heb 4:12).

3. This is the Gospel of the Lord. (The Liturgy of the Word)

Not by bread alone does man live, but by every word that comes from the mouth of the LORD. (Dt 8:3)

God is always speaking to man, but man rarely listens. This passage reminds us that the Word of God is necessary for life, as necessary as bread, yet we still fail to listen attentively. Even worse, we often plug our ears to be sure we don't hear.

The author of the Letter to the Hebrews reminds us of our very special duty to listen because of the speaker: "In times past, God spoke in partial and various ways to our ancestors through the prophets; in these last days, he spoke to us through a son" (Heb 1:1-2).

God spoke in one historical moment through His Son. He still speaks through His Son: His Son's body, the Church. The Church, in the person of the Holy Father and an ecumenical council, challenges modern men and women and their attitudes, in imitation of the

Old Testament prophets. Individual Christians have also been given the courage to speak a prophetic word against unjust and intolerable national policies and have received the reward for prophecy: suffering. Is it that we simply don't want God to speak at all?

The prophets were murdered and so was the Son. Listen to Jesus' lament, for example: "Jerusalem, Jerusalem, you who kill the prophets and stone those sent to you, how many times I yearned to gather your children together, as a hen gathers her young under her wings, but you were unwilling!" (Mt 23:37). This indicates the vigor with which humanity has repeatedly refused to listen to "every word that comes from the mouth of the Lord." We must begin to listen if we want to live; without the Word of God, we will die of starvation.

4. Praise to you, Lord Jesus Christ. (Liturgy of the Word, response to the reading of the Gospel)

"Speak, for your servant is listening." (1 Sm 3:10b)

The Scriptures are shot through with examples of various calls of the Lord and the responses they elicited. We too can learn from each one. Abraham answered the call and left his homeland in loving obedience. The prophets risked their very lives to proclaim God's Word to a people who would rather not have heard it. Mary's response changed the course of world events: "Behold, I am the handmaid of the Lord. May it be done to me according to your word" (Lk 1:38).

God is calling you today to do something significant to further His kingdom here on earth. It may not be totally earth-shattering, but if each Christian fully responded, we would have that "new heaven and new earth" foretold in the Book of Revelation (cf. 21:1), for the Kingdom would have come: "Then I saw a new heaven and a new earth. The former heaven and the former earth had passed away, and the sea was no more."

Is this our response today? "But one by one, they all began to excuse themselves . . ." (Lk 14:18).

Or are we attentive to hear His voice and obey? "Speak, for your servant is listening" (1 Sam 3:10).

Which will be your response to the Gospel?

5. A reading from the holy gospel . . . . (Liturgy of the Word)

> *How beautiful upon the mountains*
> *are the feet of him who brings glad tidings,*
> *Announcing peace, bearing good news,*
> *announcing salvation, and saying to Zion,*
> *"Your God is King!"* (Is 52:7)

How beautiful, then, were the feet of Jesus. He brought us the glad tidings of the Gospel, His incredibly Good News that we are the children of God whom He loves and wishes to save. This is the news men and women always wanted to hear and now that they have heard it, it seems too good to be true, too much to believe.

But Jesus persisted in preaching that message, for He

had no other, and He tried in many convincing ways to show that the God of love proclaimed was at work in people's lives.

People need to hear these glad tidings more than ever before. Jesus, too, must still proclaim the Gospel—through the Church, through you. People who are broken by poverty and injustice need to hear of a God who tries those He loves: "Not only that, but we even boast of our afflictions, knowing that affliction produces endurance, and endurance, proven character, and proven character, hope . . ." (Rom 5:3-4). Men and women who see life as so much suffering that joy is impossible need to hear of the Jesus Who triumphed over suffering and even death.

To us Christians have been revealed the mysteries of the kingdom of God: ". . . knowledge of the mysteries of the kingdom of heaven has been granted to you. . . ." (Mt 13:11). However, we were also given a commission and a challenge: "What I say to you in the darkness, speak in the light; what you hear whispered, proclaim on the housetops" (Mt 10:27).

6. **May the Words of the Gospel wipe away our sins.** (Liturgy of the Word, words of the ordained minister, recited inaudibly, after he kisses the Book of the Gospels)

A satan rose up against Israel, and he enticed David into taking a census of Israel. (1 Chr 21:1)

David has not been the only person in history to fall into the trap of the numbers game. Many modern

Catholics have succumbed to the polling technique of defining doctrine. We are told that a majority of American Catholics favor artificial contraception, or that a high percentage see nothing wrong with premarital intercourse, or that an increasing number do not accept papal infallibility.

At times, the statistics have been created by careful phrasing of questions to elicit a particular response. At other times, the statistics are honest reflections of popular beliefs. However, our Lord never determined that doctrine be maintained or abandoned on the basis of the latest public opinion poll. On the contrary, He held to His positions even if it meant the loss of all His followers:

> "It is the spirit that gives life, while the flesh is of no avail. The words I have spoken to you are spirit and life. But there are some of you who do not believe." Jesus knew from the beginning the ones who would not believe and the one who would betray him. And he said, "For this reason I have told you that no one can come to me unless it is granted him by my Father."
>
> As a result of this, many [of] his disciples returned to their former way of life and no longer accompanied him. (Jn 6:63-66)

Christ's yardstick was the truth of God's Word and revelation, and not the degree of public acceptance.

David was impressed by numbers; God is not. Neither should we in the Church, lest it cause us to sin by rejecting the Truth.

7. **Glory to you, Lord.** (Liturgy of the Word)

> *"For what great nation is there that has gods so close to it as the* LORD, *our God, is to us whenever we call on him?"* (Dt 4:7)

What a wonderful and consoling thought which should provide any Christian with an overflowing store of faith and hope in the face of any trial! Israel experienced it as heirs to the Jewish heritage, and we experience it as children of God in Christ.

For the Israelites, it was not boastful pride or arrogance which prompted this assertion, but an overwhelming confidence in God grounded in their concrete experience of life lived with God. If the Jews could attest to this nearness of God in the Old Testament, what shall we say when God drew so close to us in Jesus that He became one of us? Nor did God only dwell among us during one historical era; He continues to do so whenever we proclaim His Gospel of love or celebrate the sacraments of His enduring presence. He promised this, and we know God is faithful to His promises: "And behold, I am with you always, until the end of the age" (Mt 28:20).

Besides a spirit of gratitude, each Christian should have within himself an urge to spread the Good News of God's nearness with others who do not share in this utterly fantastic relationship. It was precisely this realization and desire which has accounted for the Church's missionary thrust in every generation. We can do no less today.

Questions for Group Discussion

1. Having studied the Liturgy of the Word and its important place in the Mass, discuss why the Roman Catholic Church can be correctly called a "Bible Church."

2. How are the First Reading and the Gospel related?

3. What are the three signs of special reverence shown to the gospel? Why is it treated in this way? Discuss.

4. Why is the preaching of the homily limited to an ordained minister?

5. How does the Creed function as a link between the Liturgy of the Word and the Liturgy of the Eucharist? Discuss.

CHAPTER THREE

THE PERFECT AND ACCEPTABLE SACRIFICE: THE LITURGY OF THE EUCHARIST

The Perfect and Acceptable Sacrifice: The Liturgy of the Eucharist

WE NOW MOVE INTO the second major part of the Mass. Historically, it has been referred to by a variety of names: The Mass Proper (in the sense that this is the heart of the matter); the Mass of the Faithful (since originally only the baptized in the state of grace could attend this portion); the Liturgy of the Eucharist (because this is the part in which the eucharistic Christ is actually made present). It extends from the Preparation of the Gifts through the Post-Communion Prayer. For the sake of clarity, however, we shall leave the Communion Rite for the next chapter of this book.

THE ALTAR

The altar is the focus of attention from this moment onward; whereas, the pulpit or lectern held the central

69

position during the Liturgy of the Word. It is significant that what is presently under consideration is indeed an altar. By this I mean that it is a sacred object used for the offering of a sacrifice.

Some have attempted to change its designation to that of a table, upon which a meal is eaten. However, the primary activity which occurs on it is the offering of the Eucharistic Sacrifice—a point to which we shall return later.

In speaking of the altar, it might also be well to discuss the question of the direction faced by the celebrant, since some confusion seems to exist in the minds of not a few people, priests and faithful alike. Some speak about Vatican II having decreed that the altars should be "turned around." To tell the truth, the Council never said any such thing, nor did any subsequent liturgical legislation at the universal level.

Interestingly enough, many places (especially in Spain, France, and Germany) had Mass "facing the people" decades before Vatican II. The "old Mass" could always be celebrated that way, and the best proof of it is that the papal altar in St. Peter's Basilica in Rome was so constructed in the sixteenth century that the Pope had people on all four sides of the altar.

What the liturgical documents of Vatican II advocated was a free-standing altar (one not attached to the back wall). The reason cited was to enable the celebrant to circle the altar completely when he incensed it. Some modern liturgists speak disparagingly of a Mass celebrated with "the priest's back to the people," but a more accurate description is Mass "facing eastward" (*ad Orientem*), toward the rising sun. In that style, priests and people all face the same direction.

For the priest to face the people has both advantages and disadvantages. The biggest liability is that too strong an emphasis can be placed on the celebrant—turning the Sacrifice of the Mass into a kind of drama with the priest as the principal actor. Or the misimpression can be created that it is a dialogue between priest and people. The Sacrifice of the Mass, however, is neither. It is the perfect and acceptable sacrifice of the Son to the Father, made present to us under sacramental signs.

To reap the assets of the priest facing the people—such as greater visibility—a celebrant needs to be conscious of the difficulties and thus seek to minimize them. For instance, he should not stare into the congregation during the Eucharistic Prayer, but should keep his gaze fixed either on the altar or on heaven.

Although universal law does not mandate that the Sacrifice of the Mass face the people, many bishops have called for the practice in their dioceses. This, however, should not lead to the destruction of old "high altars"—especially if they are true works of art. Much less should it suggest a cheap, uninspiring imitation stuck between the old altar and the congregation. If an altar is erected to face the people, it should be of the highest quality, befitting the worship of Almighty God, and in keeping with the architectural style of the sanctuary's original construction.

PREPARATION OF THE GIFTS

As to the Rite of Preparation of the Gifts, if a deacon is present, he brings the chalice to the altar, laying out the corporal (see Appendix Three for definition of the corporal) and removing the chalice veil.

If there is no deacon, these tasks are performed by the acolytes, who must be boys or men. This rule reflects the Church's understanding that the ministry of the acolyte is preliminary to ordination; and in a certain sense, the acolyte's service at the altar is an extension of the priest's ministry.

At the same time, the ushers (who may be male or female) take up the collection, and the congregation or choir sings a hymn related to the season, the feast, or the offering of the gifts.

The Offertory collection has roots in both the Hebrew liturgy and in that of the early Church. From the beginning, believers offered their "first fruits" to the Lord, whether of the fields or the flocks. In fact, the reader will recall that the first murder—that of Abel by his brother Cain—recorded in sacred Scripture was connected with notions of worthy and unworthy sacrifices (Gn 4).

The underlying concept of sacrificial gifts is grounded in the insight of the great Jewish thinker Rabbi Abraham Heschel: "All that we own we owe." That realization should motivate one to give sacrificially to the Church.

PRESENTATION AND OFFERING OF THE GIFTS

In the early days of Christianity, the first fruits were brought by the people to serve as thank offerings. They helped provide sustenance for the priest and, most especially, provided the elements necessary for the Eucharist—bread and wine. As the circumstances of life changed, gifts of money replaced these, except for the symbolic presentation of bread and wine to be used in the specific Eucharistic celebration underway.

The gifts are brought to the altar in procession by representatives of the congregation—a very ancient practice but one which fell into disuse in the Middle Ages. It appears that the Fathers of the Council of Trent had intended to restore it to the liturgy, but were prevailed upon not to do so because of negative reactions to having money associated with liturgical services. This was probably a result of the scandal caused by the sale of indulgences in the late Middle Ages.

The practice was re-introduced, however, in the liturgical renewal of Vatican II. It might be well to observe that only bread and wine and the collection may be included in the Offertory procession. At times inappropriate, "symbolic" gifts have been used—such as a football before a big game or a textbook at the outset of the academic year. These are not in keeping with the point of this ceremony. Furthermore, it is quite improper to offer to God "symbolically" what one intends to take back when the liturgy is over!

The Question of Mass Stipends. Perhaps this is also the moment to touch on Mass stipends. Most Catholics have, at least on occasion, gone to the rectory for a Mass card for a deceased friend. We know that the fruits of the Mass can be applied toward the welfare of either the living or the dead and that, in truth, every Mass is offered for the needs of the whole Church and the whole world. What, then, is involved in having a Mass said for a particular intention? Even more critical, is the giving and receiving of a Mass stipend an example of simony?

We must be perfectly clear here. A Mass is never bought; rather, an offering is made to the priest who celebrates the Mass. The financial gift has two effects: It associates the individual with that particular Mass in a unique manner; it contributes to the support of the priest who makes his living from the altar. Both aspects have ample scriptural warrant. Consider, for example, Leviticus 7—one among many Old Testament Scriptures—which direct that the priests are to receive a portion of certain ritual sacrifices offered to God:

> The descendant of Aaron who offers up the blood and fat of the peace offering shall have the right leg as his portion, ... This is the priestly share from the oblations of the LORD, allotted to Aaron and his sons on the day he called them to be the priests of the LORD; on the day he anointed them the LORD ordered

the Israelites to give them this share by a perpetual ordinance throughout their generations. (vv. 33, 35-36)

Finally, if every human being is prayed for at every Mass, why a Mass for an individual or special intention? The rationale is simple—it is an intense personalizing of the remembrance and application of the fruits of Christ's redemptive sacrifice. It is not unlike the difference between deciding to pray for one's whole family in a general kind of way and specifically interceding for certain members by name.

As the gifts are brought to the altar, the priest or deacon receives them. The bread which is offered must be made of unleavened wheat and water, with no additives (which would render the sacrament invalid). The Church of the West has always opted for unleavened bread, to show the connection between the Eucharist and the Passover, while many of the Churches of the East use leavened bread to emphasize the resurrection and to highlight the discontinuity between the Eucharist and the Passover—or better yet, to show how the Eucharist surpasses the Passover in significance or efficacy.

The priest presents the bread to the Father in words based on a prayer which our Lord Himself used at the Last Supper: "Blessed is the Lord our God, Ruler of the universe, Who causes bread to come forth from the earth." This prayer calls to mind the Old Testament Scripture: "For every man, moreover, to eat and drink and enjoy the fruit of all his labor is a gift of God" (Eccl 3:13).

It is worth remarking that in English the breads used for the Eucharist are called "hosts," derived from the Latin *hostia*, which means "victim." The victimhood of Christ is thus underscored even in the name and highlighted by embossing onto the hosts symbols of the Lord's passion and death.

The deacon or priest pours wine into the chalice and a drop of water. This mixture of wine and water was the usual manner of taking wine in the Mediterranean region, but it has also acquired important symbolic connotations: The wine stands for Christ and the water for humanity, whose hope is to be lost in Christ.

The priest then offers the wine, again in words reminiscent of the Passover: "Blessed is the Creator of the Fruit of the vine." One is reminded of Jesus' own words at the Last Supper: "Take this and share it among yourselves; for I tell you [that] from this time on I shall not drink of the fruit of the vine until the kingdom of God comes" (Lk 22:17-18).

It should be observed that the Gnostic heretics refused to use wine in the Eucharist because of their austerity and distaste for anything which could bring joy or pleasure. A Eucharist without wine, however, is not the Eucharist since it fails to reproduce what Christ did.

The prayers which accompany the offering of the bread and wine are blessings in the Jewish sense of the word, that is, prayers of praise and thanksgiving to the Lord for His gifts, which are now returned to Him. The prayers focus our attention on the natural origin of the gifts, but most especially on their destiny as "the Bread of life" and "our spiritual drink."

The Offertory prayers of the "old Mass" were beautiful, but a bit too sacrificial for this point in the liturgy. They tended to blur the fact that our real act of offering occurs during the Eucharistic Prayer, when we offer not bread and wine but Christ Himself. The current prayers are more muted in this regard, all the while pointing toward the sacrifice-to-come.

In solemn liturgies, the priest incenses the gifts for what they are—the works of creation and human labor—and for what they will become—the Body and Blood of Christ. (To signify this at the elevation of the sacred Species in solemn liturgies, yet another incensing occurs.) The priest walks around the altar incensing it as an act of homage toward Christ, Who is represented by the altar. Then those involved in worship are honored with incense as well, as God's holy ministers and His people. All are recognized as temples of the Holy Spirit by virtue of incorporation into the body of Christ through Baptism and Confirmation.

Following these rites, the priest washes his hands; it is not, by the way, an optional rite. This ceremomy is simply a humble admission that he shares in the lot common to all the sinful children of Adam and Eve. In the early Church, this act had a practical necessity to it since the priest's hands would have been soiled by contact with the gifts of grain, fruits, or animals. Today its purpose is to stress the need for the priest to be cleansed interiorly, in order to offer the Eucharistic Sacrifice worthily.

That having been said, it is helpful to underline that the validity of any sacrament does not depend on the holiness of the particular minister who officiates. That matter was definitively settled by the Church in the Donatist Controversy of the fifth century. Were the situation otherwise, no one could ever be certain of having received a valid sacrament since no one has knowledge of the souls of others. Beyond that, though, the essential doctrine to remember is that the principal celebrant in every sacrament is Jesus Christ, and not the human instrument.

The liturgical assembly is now invited to join the priest in praying the "our sacrifice may be acceptable to God, the almighty Father." The prayer is lovely, but the English text has two regrettable omissions, with important theological implications. First, the Latin speaks of the sacrifice as *ac meum ac vestrum* ("yours and mine"), while the English speaks of it as "ours"—an unfortunate merging of the sacrifice of the ordained priest with that of the whole priestly people. To be sure, the sacrifice is one, and both priest and faithful are united in the act of offering it. But the relationship between the priest and the sacrifice is qualitatively different: A priest can offer the Eucharist without a congregation with sufficient reason; a congregation without a priest can never do so.

Second, the people's response in Latin refers to *ecclesiae suae sanctae* ("his holy Church"), but the adjective "holy" is eliminated in the English. This leaves out an important reality that deserves emphasis—that although the Church is composed of sinners, in her corporate identity she is the sinless bride of Christ. And this occurs most definitively when she offers the Eucharistic Sacrifice under the headship of her bridegroom.

The Eucharist is indeed *the* wedding feast of the Lamb, as the Book of Revelation reminds us: "Then the angel said to me, 'Write this: Blessed are those who have been called to the wedding feast of the Lamb.' And he said to me, 'These words are true; they come from God' " (Rv 19:9). Only the mystery of a sinless Church (albeit with sinful persons in her midst) can sanctify her members—the goal of the Christian life in general and of the sacraments in particular.

Finally, the priest recites or chants the Prayer over the Gifts, which is a request that the Lord look favorably on our sacrifice. All is now in readiness to enter into the heart of the sacred mysteries—the Eucharistic Prayer.

THE STRUCTURE OF THE EUCHARISTIC PRAYER

If the central act of Christian worship is the offering of the Eucharistic Sacrifice, its centerpiece is the anaphora (taken from the Greek *anaphorein*, meaning "to offer up"). It is also known as the Eucharistic Prayer or the Canon. Historically, one finds not a single prayer

but a single format. This format came about as the
Jewish *berakahs* or traditional thanksgiving prayers
were Christianized.

The structure of the Eucharistic Prayer is rather
straightforward and, in general, common to the liturgy
of the East and West alike. The prayer opens with an
introductory dialogue and a hymn of praise (Preface
and *Sanctus*). The narrative leading up to the Consecration combines Gospel texts and St. Paul's account
to the Corinthians, in order to re-enact the drama of the
Lord's gift of Himself at the Last Supper. Essential
elements include the invocation of the Holy Spirit (the
epiclesis) to sanctify and transform the gifts of bread and
wine into the Body and Blood of Christ, and the memorial, commemoration, or remembrance (the *anamnesis*),
which renders Jesus' past action present:

> Then he took a cup, gave thanks, and said, "Take this
> and share it among yourselves; for I tell you [that]
> from this time on I shall not drink of the fruit of the
> vine until the kingdom of God comes." Then he took
> the bread, said the blessing, broke it, and gave it to
> them, saying, "This is my body, which will be given
> for you; do this in memory of me." And likewise the
> cup after they had eaten, saying, "This cup is the new
> covenant in my blood, which will be shed for
> you."(Lk 22:17-20)

This notion of memorial is at the heart of biblical or
Jewish worship. The great liturgist, Dom Gregory Dix,
spoke of this as "the 'recalling' before God of the one

sacrifice of Christ in all its accomplished fullness so that it is here and now operative by its effects in the souls of the redeemed."

The Eucharistic Prayer is brought to a conclusion with the doxology or hymn of praise of the Father through, with, and in Christ, and in the unity of the Holy Spirit. Thus the prayer begins and ends with praise.

It should be noted that although the Eucharistic Prayer is always addressed to the First Person of the Blessed Trinity, it is Christo-centric as well—in that its action is advanced in reference to the Second Person of the Blessed Trinity. That is, of course, why its recitation—or better, its proclamation—is reserved to the priest as the *alter Christus* ("another Christ").

Now we turn to a discussion of the four Eucharistic Prayers.

THE FIRST EUCHARISTIC PRAYER

Of the four Eucharistic Prayers currently in universal use in the Roman Rite (as a matter of fact, there are also three Eucharistic Prayers for Children's Masses and two for Masses of Reconciliation, but we shall not consider them here), the First Eucharistic Prayer or Roman Canon holds pride of place. It is referred to as Roman because it originated in Rome at the end of the fourth century and came into its present form during the pontificate of St. Gregory the Great in the seventh century. It has not changed significantly since then.

Although it is not the most ancient Canon (Eucharistic Prayer II is), it has been in continuous use the longest. It is called the "Canon" because it is basically unchangeable, except for special inserts for the celebration of principal feasts or certain sacraments.

Eucharistic Prayer I consists of fifteen prayers which Enrico Mazza has referred to as "tiles in a mosaic." Each tile can be regarded separately and thus appreciated, or the tiles can be reviewed in relation to each other, so that the total picture emerges. In our analysis of this prayer, we should seek to do both.

First, the liturgical revisions following Vatican II specify that the Christological endings and their accompanying "Amens" may be omitted from the fifteen prayers that comprise the Canon, so as to make clearer its unity. There is a logic to these clearly delineated parts in this prayer.

For example, in the ancient Church, the homily was more a verse-by-verse commentary on the Scripture readings than its modern counterpart, which endeavors to pull together the various strands in such a way that an essay on a central theme is produced. That is why a line-by-line investigation of the Roman Canon would yield the best results. So, with missal in hand, we should begin.

Throughout, the priest speaks in the first person plural, using "we." This has the effect of locating him within the community and at the same time at the head of the body—*in persona Christi* (the "person of Christ"). Only at the words of institution does he slip into the first person singular, as he "puts on Christ" in a unique manner (hence, the necessity of a male priest to accomplish this task), becoming Christ in such wise as almost to set aside (if that were possible) his identification with the Church.

The other pronoun to notice is "you," addressed to the Father. The Eucharistic Prayer is not a dialogue between priest and people. Therefore, it should be obvious that the priest's gaze (as mentioned earlier) should not be on the congregation but on the Person to whom the prayer is directed. Even when the celebrant speaks words which are addressed by the Lord to His disciples (and hence one might conclude that looking at the people would be opportune), the rubrics direct otherwise.

What makes our prayer effective is that our act of "praise and thanksgiving" is made "through Jesus Christ your Son," through whom we also ask the Father to "accept and bless these gifts we offer you in sacrifice."

The notion of sacrifice is basic to all religions, and hence its prominence in Catholicism and our most important act of worship. Yet the Protestant Reformers endeavored to strip the liturgy of sacrificial overtones to eliminate the priesthood, for sacrifice and priesthood go together. Certain Protestants today have an allergic reaction to the suggestion that the Eucharist is a sacrifice, fearing—they say—that it obscures the once-and-for-all sacrifice of Christ.

Such concerns, however, are moot when one realizes that the Eucharistic Sacrifice is offered only in union with Christ's all-sufficient sacrifice on Calvary, without which the Eucharist would have as much or as little lasting value as its Old Testament prototypes seen in the sacrifices of Abel, Abraham, and Melchizedek—which are alluded to after the Consecration of the bread and wine.

Since Christ's self-offering on the cross is the preeminent and eternal act of intercession (now celebrated in the liturgy), intercessory prayer is at the very heart of the Canon. This is entirely appropriate and in no way a duplication of the General Intercessions. Note that the first objective of prayer is the "holy catholic Church." The use of the word "catholic" here does not connote universality as much as it points to the "Great Church," in the sense of the undivided and sect-free body of Christ. The English translation is unfortunate in its use of the impersonal pronoun "it," rather than the personal pronoun "she" or "her." At root, the Church is properly seen as a person, namely, the bride of Christ and our mother. Consider these two Pauline Scriptures, for example:

> Wives should be subordinate to their husbands as to the Lord. For the husband is head of his wife just as Christ is head of the church, he himself the savior of the body. . . . Husbands, love your wives, even as Christ loved the church and handed himself over for her to sanctify her, cleansing her by the bath of water with the word, that he might present to himself the church in splendor, without spot or wrinkle or any such thing, that she might be holy and without blemish. (Eph 5:22-23, 25-27)

But the Jerusalem above is freeborn, and she is our mother.

For it is written:

"Rejoice, you barren one who bore no children;
break forth and shout, you who were not in labor;
for more numerous are the children of the deserted
   one
than of her who has a husband." (Gal 4:26-27)

In the intercessions, the first remembered by name is the Pope as universal pastor, and the local bishop, who presides over the diocese, which is a microcosm of the Church Universal. The reason for their inclusion at this point is that their primary function is to safeguard "the catholic faith that comes to us from the apostles." Without the apostolic faith, no true Eucharist is possible.

Then the Latin text uses a series of verbs in an attempt to fill out the implications of biblical "shalom"— that fullness of life, love, unity, harmony, joy, and wholeness which is God's gift to his people. The English is somewhat impoverished as we limply ask the Lord to "grant (the Church) peace and unity throughout the world."

The next to benefit from the Eucharist are the living, faithful members of Christ's Church. We pray not only for ourselves but also for "those who are dear to us." Lest our view be restricted to this earthly sphere, our horizon is expanded to include the Church in heaven. Heading the procession is the Blessed Virgin Mary—

Mother of Christ and Mother of the Church—followed by her spouse St. Joseph (the addition of whose name by Pope John XXIII stunned the Council Fathers at the conclusion of the first session of Vatican II); the twelve apostles; twelve other special witnesses to Christ, including four early martyrs, three popes, and five patron saints of Roman basilicas (Remember: this *is* the *Roman* Canon!).

The next two prayers beseech God to sanctify the gifts on the altar, so that they become the eucharistic presence of the Lord, which can then confer on us God's "peace in this life, (and) save us from final damnation." Significantly, this is the only Canon which speaks directly of hell.

Then come the words of institution or consecration, followed by the *anamnesis* or prayer of remembrance. In biblical theology, these prayers taken together would constitute the central elements by which the Lord's sacramental presence is effected. In Hebrew thought categories (necessary to adopt for a healthy liturgical spirituality), sacred memory leads to sacred reality.

Unlike us modern Westerners, when Jews remember or recall God's salvific activities of the past, those events happen all over again for those who bring them to mind. It is against this background that the Church can declare with complete confidence that her eucharistic action is indeed a liturgical reenactment of Christ's death on Calvary and not a blasphemous effort to "add to" His saving death and resurrection. However, the distinction is only possible where a biblical notion of *anamnesis* or remembrance is in place.

Congregational participation is evoked by the memorial acclamation as the people are urged to "proclaim *the* mystery of faith." And what is that mystery? Nothing less than the Lord's paschal mystery sacramentally celebrated in these rites. It is significant that three of the four acclamations of the people address Christ directly—an implicit acknowledgment of His presence now on the altar.

After the memorial acclamation, the Church prays for the acceptability of her sacrifice in God's sight, in a prayer which is a beautiful reminder of the divine freedom to accept or reject our offerings. God cannot be magically manipulated by us. Of course, the wholly marvelous truth is that by Jesus' free and loving decision, He has chosen to come among us under the appearances of bread and wine when in obedience to His command, we "do this in memory of" Him. Then, as one preface puts it, the Father "see(s) and love(s) in us what (he) see(s) and love(s) in Christ." God accepts the Church's sacrifice because it is Christ's.

The same prayer stirs happy and holy memories of the sacrifices of the Old Covenant, which were acceptable because the gifts offered and the persons offering them were mirror images of each other in holiness and obedience to the Lord. As such, those men of old serve as models for us today—concrete sources of encouragement to be as holy as the gifts we offer and receive.

The prayer that follows is a lovely petition that Almighty God's angel "may take this sacrifice to your altar in heaven." Thus is it envisioned that the liturgy of earth and heaven are united in much the same way that the *Sanctus* sees "heaven and earth (being) filled with your glory." It is a powerful reminder that what we celebrate and worship here in signs will reach its fulfillment in the life of heaven. We have God's incredible promise on that, in the words of St. Paul:

At present we see indistinctly, as in a mirror, but then face to face. At present I know partially; then I shall know fully, as I am fully known. So faith, hope, love remain, these three; but the greatest of these is love. (1 Cor 13:12-13)

Our list of intercessions and remembrances is now filled out as the prayers for the dead balance out the earlier prayers for the living—and as we commemorate the saints in glory. (It should be noted that of the fifteen saints venerated at this point in the liturgy, seven are women.) By looking upon the saints in glory, we are immediately brought face to face with our sinfulness, yet remain hopeful since "we trust in your mercy and love."

In a gesture of repentance, the priest strikes his breast and then in a manner at once humble and realistic, the Church entreats: "Do not consider what we truly deserve, but grant us your forgiveness." God's mercy, like salvation itself, is never earned. It is always a gift—the offer of which is renewed in each celebration of the Eucharistic Sacrifice.

With all the tiles presented for careful examination, what emerges? A magnificent mosaic, as Mazza has suggested. The First Eucharistic Prayer is a masterpiece of theological depth and literary excellence, appealing to heart and mind at one and the same time. When confronted with the majesty and graciousness of God in such striking symbols, what else should the people do but say, "Amen"?

THE SECOND EUCHARISTIC PRAYER

The Second Eucharistic Prayer has the most ancient origins of the four. It is also the simplest and the shortest. This prayer is probably the best known today, more due to its brevity than its antiquity, if the truth be told.

When the decision was made to recite the Canon audibly and in the vernacular, many liturgists argued that alternatives to the Roman Canon would be necessary to avoid monotony. One of the first Eucharistic Prayers they thought attractive as an alternative was that of Hippolytus, a Roman priest who died as a martyr in A.D. 235. His "Apostolic Tradition" contains a Eucharistic Prayer used during the Mass of a newly ordained bishop. Although celebrants were free to extemporize the liturgy in the early Church, one can see already by this date a concern for set formulas.

As the anaphora of St. Hippolytus was re-worked for modern use, it was shortened to remove the specifically paschal overtones of the original (the episcopal consecration had obviously occurred during Eastertide). Also the prayer's institution or consecration narrative was edited to coincide with that of the Roman

Canon, leading to a unified eucharistic theology among all the Eucharistic Prayers. The practical advantage here was that concelebrants could then recite the words of consecration from memory. The original intention of these early liturgists was that this prayer would be primarily geared to weekday Masses of lesser solemnity or when pastoral need dictated a shorter celebration.

Ordinarily, the priest should use the preface proper to this Eucharistic Prayer—although this is not required as it is for the Fourth Eucharistic Prayer. This preface sets the tone for the whole prayer by indicating that our act of thanksgiving (i.e., Eucharist) is offered "through your beloved Son, Jesus Christ." Drawing on the ancient Hebrew literary form of inclusion, the prayer ends as it begins—with the hope that our praise of God would always be accomplished "through your Son, Jesus Christ." Thus this framework is thoroughly Christological.

The "beloved Son" is the one to whom believers are directed to give ear, as the Father commanded at the Lord's Baptism. He is the Word spoken from all eternity and incarnate in the fullness of time, reminiscent of the Jesus introduced in the Prologue to St. John's Gospel:

> In the beginning was the Word,
>   and the Word was with God,
>   and the Word was God.
> He was in the beginning with God.
> All things came to be through him,
>   and without him nothing came to be. (1:1-3)

Another Johannine touch is the mention of Jesus "open(ing) his arms on the cross": "And just as Moses lifted up the serpent in the desert, so must the Son of Man be lifted up, ..." (Jn 3:14). This stretching out of His hands is simultaneously the priestly gesture of prayer and the shepherdly gathering in of the flock in a loving embrace.

The anaphora stresses the voluntary nature of Christ's self-sacrifice—another Johannine theme. Because Jesus is the "beloved Son"— the "Word" of creation, the Priest, and the Shepherd—His actions have eternal, saving consequences, namely, that He has "won for (the Father) a holy people." The moving image of Jesus as the Good Shepherd bears reflection here:

> I am the good shepherd, and I know mine and mine know me, just as the Father knows me and I know the Father; and I will lay down my life for the sheep. ... This is why the Father loves me, because I lay down my life in order to take it up again. No one takes it from me, but I lay it down on my own.
>
> (Jn 10:14-15, 17-18a)

A lesser personage could never effect the reconciliation of heaven and earth, symbolized in the recitation of the *Sanctus*.

Picking up the notion of divine holiness, the Eucharistic Prayer acknowledges that God is "holy indeed." This is not one quality among many in the Godhead; it is the very essence of divinity. With that in mind, the Church invokes the Third Person of the Blessed Trinity—the Spirit of holiness—to "come upon these gifts (of bread and wine) to make them holy." Through-out the Scriptures, it is always God who sanctifies acceptable sacrifices made in His Name.

Later, we will pray that those holy gifts will, in turn, make holy those who receive them—just as the priests in the Temple of Jerusalem pleaded to God for the removal of the sins of those who brought sacrificial offerings. This invocation of the Spirit or *epiclesis* is Trinitarian in scope: It beseeches the Father to send forth the Spirit to transform the gifts into the Body and Blood of the Son, thus calling for the fresh infusion of the life of the Trinity in the hearts of the faithful. A second invocation (after the Consecration) calls for the unity of all communicants as the special work of the Eucharist and the Spirit.

Turning to the Consecration, since the words of institution have been discussed for the Roman Canon and are basically the same for all four Eucharistic Prayers, some comments on secondary aspects of this sacred moment may be worthwhile.

First, according to the General Instruction of the Roman Missal, the posture for the congregation from the epiclesis or invocation to the memorial acclamation is kneeling as a sign of adoration. The bishops of the United States received an indult to have the people kneel for the entire Eucharistic Prayer. An indult is a favor granted by the Holy See to bishops which permits them to do something not otherwise allowed.

The thinking behind the request was never clearly spelled out, but it seems that some liturgists main-tained that kneeling for the limited span mandated by the Missal "over-emphasized" the Consecration! Yet again, some bishops felt that the then venerable American tradition of kneeling for the whole time should be retained. Whatever the original rationale, liturgical law for this country requires the congregation to kneel for the entire Eucharistic Prayer—regrettably noted more often in the breach than in the observance.

Second, although the priest echoes the words of Jesus at the Last Supper, he does not mimic Him. Therefore, the host is not broken at that precise moment. Rather, the breaking of the bread is deferred to the *Agnus Dei* ("the Lamb of God"), where the connection between the Lord's redemptive sacrifice (the broken Body) and the sharing in the "one Bread and one Cup" in Holy Communion is more apparent.

Third, for those who argue that the Eucharist is *primarily* a meal, Jesus' prayer over the wine argues to the contrary: "When supper was *ended*, he took the cup...." Jesus' action after the meal reinforces that the Mass is fundamentally a sacrifice—like those of the Old Testament—which includes a partaking of the sacrifice to signify participation in the effects of the sacrifice: namely, redemption and reconciliation.

Fourth, some people have expressed concern that the English translation of *pro multis* as "for all" does violence to the traditional doctrine of salvation. The Latin *pro multis* is properly rendered as "for *the* many," which is a Hebrew idiom, meaning "everyone" or "all." Therefore, it is quite appropriate to say that Jesus' Blood was "shed for you and for *all*."

Does not this square completely with the Scripture

which asserts that God "wills everyone to be saved and to come to knowledge of the truth" (1 Tm 2:4)? Christ did indeed pour out His Blood for all. Unfortunately, not all will benefit from His saving love because they reject it and Him.

To resume our study of Eucharistic Prayer II, we look to the *anamnesis* or prayer of memory in which the act of memorial is linked to the Lord's paschal mystery, thus bridging the gap of time in an eternal present—God's "time." Like the Roman Canon, this Eucharistic Prayer sounds the note of human unworthiness to approach the all-holy God, stated in positive language: "We thank you for counting us worthy to stand in your presence and serve you." It is only God's forgiving and loving decision which justifies humanity.

Prayer II is rounded out with intercession made for the Church, especially the Bishop of Rome and the local bishop who are guarantors of unity for the "Church throughout the world." Also remembered at the altar of the Lord are deceased Christians, as well as "all the departed." The hope is that all redeemed humanity would be brought into the life of heaven where the Blessed Virgin and the other saints already behold the face of God in glory.

This anaphora begins and ends in eternity, and rightly so, for the Eucharist is the feast of the *eschaton* or end-time. It enables those who share in it here on earth to experience a foretaste of heaven by manifesting the joy, peace, and unity of the kingdom in this disordered world. The Eucharist anticipates the end-time in a two-fold movement: Through the liturgical re-enactment of the Lord's passion, death, and resurrection, God comes to us in a unique manner, which then has the effect of drawing us to Him—now and unto eternity.

THE THIRD EUCHARISTIC PRAYER

The Third Eucharistic Prayer is a completely modern composition, essentially the work of the Benedictine liturgist Cyprian Vaggagini. That does not mean, however, that it was created *ex nihilo* ("out of nothing"). On the contrary, its stress on the Eucharist as a sacrifice clearly links it up with the Roman Canon. More careful investigation also reveals connections with the Gallican and Mozarabic Rites (old French and Spanish). In keeping with the scriptural revival, biblical echoes resonate strongly throughout this anaphora.

The prayer opens with a grand sweep from the dawn of time down to the present moment. Like some of the later epistles attributed to St. Paul (Ephesians, Philippians, Colossians) and the writings of Irenaeus, this Eucharistic Prayer sees "all creation," and not just the Church or even humanity-at-large, involved with the praise of God. Furthermore, Christ is placed at the center of it all as the source of "all life, all holiness."

This Eucharistic Prayer also has a very ecclesial orientation, recounting for us how God formed a people for Himself. At the outset, we are reminded that "from age to age you gather a people to yourself." This "gathering" began when God first made the covenant with Abraham and reached its high point when His divine Son made "the new and everlasting covenant" in His Blood.

What was the purpose of God's formation of a Church? His own glory: "So that from east to west a perfect offering may be made to the glory of your name." It should be noted that this (Mal 1:11), "pure offering," envisioned by the prophet Malachi, did not consist solely in the right sacrifice being offered according to the correct ritual formulas. That is necessary, of course, but more is required—the pure gifts must represent people of pure hearts if the rite is to have any true significance.

The allusion to Malachi is sadly lost by a defective English translation. The Latin text quotes the prophet directly by indicating our desire for this sacrifice to be made "from the rising of the sun to its setting." In other words, the Eucharist is to be celebrated throughout the waking hours. That equally implies the living out of the Eucharist in one's daily life. The official translation of the International Commission on English in the Liturgy takes a temporal image (dawn to dusk) and switches it to a spatial one (east to west). Also lacking is nature's participation in the Eucharistic Sacrifice since the specific reference to the sun is dropped.

The usual invocation of the Holy Spirit follows, but with a subtle and important addition: The statement that this liturgical action of the Church occurs in obedience to Christ's "command." Most people tend to forget that the words of institution always end with the Lord's directive that His disciples do indeed remember Him precisely by re-enacting this ritual faithfully.

This realization places the Eucharist in a unique perspective and context. We do not celebrate it according to personal whim; we do it because Christ has commanded us to do so. Why would a condemned man make this His last request? Because remembering Jesus in this sacrificial rite would bring to mind everything associated with this sacred meal—the covenant, the price of sin, the love of God, the need to return that love and to share it with others. Remembering our Lord in the Eucharist is a refresher course in the basics of Gospel living. It provides a challenge to be eucharistic people as well as the strength and grace to become the same.

One should observe that the consecratory prayers (faithful to the Gospel texts) speak of the Lord's sacrificial death in the future tense: "This is my body which *will* be given up . . . This is the cup of my blood . . . It *will* be shed . . ." Our focus, then, is not exclusively or even primarily on that Last Supper with its Passover overtones, for the Passover meal was but a veiled sign or type of something far more effective and glorious, namely, the self-offering of the Lamb of God personified—the Second Person of the Blessed Trinity. Thus Holy Thursday's covenantal meal of promise is completed, sealed, and admirably fulfilled in Good Friday's covenantal sacrifice.

The prayer of remembrance has a standard and essential grammatical structure: The act of offering is dependent upon the act of memory—"calling to mind . . . we offer . . ." This is not an exercise in nit-picking but is at the very heart of true biblical worship. One does not attempt to offer the Eucharistic Sacrifice independently of the memorial of Christ's once-for-all sacrifice.

This prayer also fixes our gaze on the finish line by assuring our readiness "to greet him when he comes again." In point of fact, the present recalling (the liturgy) of a past event (the Lord's paschal mystery) prepares us to face His future coming with confidence and even with eager longing.

Like the First Eucharistic Prayer, this anaphora prays for the acceptability of our sacrifice before God and then makes an ecclesial request: "Grant that we, who are nourished by his body and blood, may be filled with his Holy Spirit, and become one body, one spirit in Christ." The Eucharist, then, has a two-fold effect—communion with the Lord and, at the very same time, communion with one another in the Church. A fruitful celebration of the Eucharist achieves both effects. As the late Archbishop Fulton J. Sheen was fond of saying, the vertical and the horizontal are joined and form a cross, which is here commemorated.

The prayer which follows asks Christ to "make us an everlasting gift to you." Feeding on Christ should make all partakers, "other Christs" in a sense. As the German proverb puts it, "a man is what he eats." Therefore, we are expected to become "an everlasting gift" to the Father because Jesus our model and pattern of holiness is just that.

Lest the task appear too awesome or out of reach, we hear mentioned several examples of members of the Church who have "made it." This prayer permits the insertion of the name of a saint who has special relevance to a particular celebration or parish community: for example, the saint of the day or patron of the parish.

This prayer is unabashed in its affirmation of the communion of saints—another indication of its strong ecclesial thrust. Not only does it speak of the "constant intercession" of the saints in glory (for all are alive in Christ, as St. Paul tells us), but then it even more boldly declares that we "rely" on this intercession. Again, the point is made that the Christian life is not something exclusively between "Jesus and me." But it is God's will that it be a communal affair. This means we are called to be actively concerned with each other's salvation and are able to assist each other through our prayers.

Although this Eucharistic Prayer would have us rejoice in our identity as members of Christ's Church, its mentality is neither narcissistic nor triumphalistic. Thus the priest entreats that just as the Eucharist makes Christians acceptable to the Father, so too would this Eucharist "advance the peace and salvation of *all* the world."

A healthy eucharistic theology always causes believers to move beyond the Church's frontiers in the works of charity and evangelization, in imitation of the Blessed Virgin Mary. After all, having received Christ into her womb, she immediately went forth to share the Good News with her cousin Elizabeth and to tend to her needs. This openness to the world is also exhibited in the commemoration of the dead where first consideration is given to departed Christians. But then we recall "all who have left this world in your friendship," thus admitting the possibility for God to save others in ways known only to Him in His wisdom and mercy.

The Eucharistic Prayer also asks Almighty God to "strengthen in faith and love your pilgrim Church on earth." Several concerns surface here. First, it is a sobering reminder that the Church is *simul justus et peccator*—the sinless bride of Christ on the one hand, yet still composed of weak, sinful human beings on the other. Therefore, she needs purification which only her Lord can accomplish.

Second, by using the term "pilgrim Church," that felicitous phrase of Vatican II, the Church places herself *in via,* "on the road." We understand, with the author of the Epistle to the Hebrews, that "here we have no lasting city" (13:14). That should not suggest that we can be uninterested in earthly affairs, but it does call for a different tone and attitude in our conduct—one which does not pretend that we have all our eggs in this earthly basket.

Third, the anaphora speaks subtly of the Church's identity when it says that this community is "your" Church. It is not a human construct—it is God's handiwork. This means our attitude toward the Church is not the same as it might be toward some multinational corporation. No, the Church is the "family you have gathered here before you."

Vatican II has been called "the Council of the

Church"; hence, it should come as no surprise that this Eucharistic Prayer composed in the Council's wake should reflect this orientation. A strong ecclesiology highlights the need for an equally strong eucharistic theology, for the Church becomes ever more clearly the body of Christ in being nourished by the Body of Christ, which is effected through the Eucharistic Prayer.

THE FOURTH EUCHARISTIC PRAYER

The Fourth Eucharistic Prayer, like the third, is a modern composition, although somewhat related to the Eastern liturgies of St. John Chrysostom and St. Basil. It renders a detailed account of salvation history and both presumes and provides solid grounding in biblical theology. The authors of this Eucharistic Prayer did not envision its use for solemnities, feasts, Sundays, Advent, or Lent because of its unchangeable preface.

An interesting side-light is that this prayer has gained ecumenical acceptance, with only minor adjustments made mostly in the intercession of the saints and prayer for the hierarchy. Who would have dreamed twenty years ago that Protestant eucharistic theology and ecumenical understanding would develop to the point that certain Protestant communions would feel comfortable reciting a Catholic Eucharistic Prayer? Granted, not all Protestants can do so or are even inclined to do so. However, when reflecting on the

Eucharist—which is a sign and cause of unity in Christ—this turn of events is genuine reason for rejoicing.

Of all the Eucharistic Prayers, this one has encountered the most difficulties in its English rendition. Two serious errors in the translation required the intervention of the Congregation for the Doctrine of the Faith. The first involved the preface, in which the Father was addressed as "the only God"—a careless mistake suggesting that only the Father is God! The second faux pas occurred after the Consecration as the priest prayed for "all who share this *bread and wine*"—an implicit denial of transsubstantiation. Cardinal Joseph Ratzinger directed the American bishops to have the liturgical books corrected, and that has been done. It must be stressed that the original Latin did not contain these heterodox statements.

This anaphora in Latin refers to the First Person of the Blessed Trinity six times as "Father," four of those times using the modifier "holy." This, of course, is intended to parallel Jesus' address to his heavenly Father at the Last Supper, where he repeatedly called on him as "holy Father" or "Father most holy." Strangely, the adjective "holy" never appears in the English.

Another problem revolves around the so-called "exclusive" or "sexist" language in this Eucharistic Prayer, such as "man" and "he." It is a testimony to the perils of vernacular liturgy that just over a decade ago—when this prayer first became available in English—that was no issue at all. Now demands are made by some (a decided but vocal minority) for changes which reflect "inclusive" language. Without embarking on a major digression, let me simply suggest that weaknesses are inherent in all languages. For example, the word "person" in the Romance languages is feminine, but no one seems to have launched a drive to eradicate its use. Needless to say, celebrants are not free to make any such changes, for the Mass is not the personal possession of any individual or group.

The preface begins the recital of *eu-angellion* ("the Good News"), leading to the response which is right and just: *eucharistia* (the good work of thanks). God's attributes are set forth at the outset: He is one, living and true. Who He is tells us something of who we are and what He expects of us, His creatures. At its conclusion, we state our belief that our act of praise and thanksgiving is united to that of the angels (above us in the created order) and brings with it all of creation below us.

This is the theology of Genesis 1 and 2 at its best, with all the peripheral concerns of creationism and biblical literalism set aside in favor of the underlying salvific truth: The human person is the pinnacle of the material creation and its steward, made just a "little less than the angels."

Speaking of angels, it is well to observe that all the anaphoras feel compelled to allude to them. Their inclusion is a reminder that reality consists of something beyond the material universe. Furthermore, their activities are exemplary for us in certain key areas: their obedience to God ("stand before you to do your will"); contemplation of God ("they look upon your splendor"); and praise of God (which they do "night and day").

The utter transcendence and majesty of God comes through powerfully in the Fourth Eucharistic Prayer, emphasizing as it does, the God who creates, redeems, and sanctifies. Voltaire said that God created man in His own image, and man has never ceased to return the compliment. The truth of that insight calls for the corrective of a heavy dose of divine transcendence.

In this Eucharistic Prayer, the recalling of all the ancient covenants prepares for the ultimate covenant which came "in the fullness of time [when] you sent your only Son to be our Savior." Those divine interventions of old similarly foreshadowed the definitive intervention in the incarnation and its extension now in space and time through the Eucharist.

Just prior to the Consecration, Eucharistic Prayer IV, speaks of: "When the time came for him . . ." "Time" is here a translation of "hora" or "hour"—the same word used dozens of times in St. John's Gospel to signal the proper moment, the time of Jesus' passion, death, and resurrection—His hour of glory. This hour is exactly what each eucharistic celebration commemorates and, in so doing, represents it. We are thus brought into the Upper Room, onto Calvary, and then back to the Upper Room to behold Him on Easter night. His hour becomes ours.

Finally, we beseech Almighty God to permit us "to enter into our heavenly inheritance." Hearing the word "inheritance," two thoughts come to mind: First, our status as adopted children through Christ's redemptive sacrifice; second, the last will and testament (or covenant) in Christ's Blood, which guarantees us the inheritance. What a loaded word, so packed with significance of eternal consequences!

The Church of the East emphasizes this dimension in a way we of the West do not. Everything about their liturgy points to another world: exquisite vestments, billowing incense, haunting *a capella* chants, sacral language (even in the vernacular). This other-worldly approach is not escapism. On the contrary, it enables believers to confront the real world with renewed vigor because the liturgy has anticipated and made present eternal realities, pointing to the end of the age and the age to come.

Our Lord transfigured Himself before Peter, James, and John, showing to them the glory to which He and they were called: The inheritance awaiting all the children of God. That experience gave them the spiritual and emotional strength to face His passion and their own. The Eucharistic Prayer should do the same for us.

SCRIPTURAL MEDITATIONS FOR THE LITURGY OF THE EUCHARIST

1. It is desirable that the participation of the faithful be expressed by members of the congregation bringing up the bread and the wine for the celebration of the Eucharist or other gifts for the needs of the Church and

the poor. (Liturgy of the Eucharist, directions for Preparation of the Gifts)

> *". . . the measure of your own freewill offering shall be in proportion to the blessing the LORD, your God, has bestowed on you."* (Dt 16:10b)

"They're always asking for money. It's just a big business." How often have you heard these statements made about the Church? Maybe you have even made them yourself. Such comments betray a cynicism unworthy of a Christian, as well as an ignorance of the facts. Allowing for the rare exception, the priest who asks for money is doing so to advance the Gospel in one apostolate or another. Let us be honest enough to concede that much.

When people refuse to contribute, are they very subtly stating that what they have is their own, and they owe thanks to no one, including God? What does it say about modern Catholics in America that they (the most affluent Catholic population of the present or past) cannot maintain the network of churches, schools, hospitals and other agencies begun with the pennies of our immigrant ancestors? How close do most Catholics come to the biblical admonition of tithing?

Yet another consideration: Maybe we are generous with our money, but is that because it can be an easy salve? What about a generosity with our time, our energy, and our talents? If you are blessed with good health, visit a hospital to encourage someone who does not share your blessing. If you are blessed with freedom and a clear conscience, seek out a prisoner whom you may be able to inspire by your interest and compassion. If you are blessed with a good family and home, go to the family which does not enjoy such happiness. Perhaps you will even open your home to them.

Your generosity will bless and enrich others—and you. Isn't that what is meant in the prayer attributed to St. Francis of Assisi when it says, "It is in giving that we receive"?

**2. Holy, holy, holy Lord, God of power and might,
heaven and earth are full of your glory.**
    Hosanna in the highest.
Blessed is he who comes in the name of the Lord.
    Hosanna in the highest. (Sanctus)

"Holy, holy, holy is the LORD of hosts!" they cried one to the other. "All the earth is filled with his glory!" At the sound of that cry, the frame of the door shook, and the house was filled with smoke. (Is 6:3-4)

There have always been some approaches to God which are woefully inadequate. One person sees God as holy but remote and distant. Another sees the universe filled with His glory, but the need for God Himself is not sufficiently stressed.

When we sing this heavenly hymn at Mass, it comes at a most significant point: The all-holy God will be on the altar in moments under the appearances of bread and wine, created things. And that is the way to view the holiness of God and the wonder of creation. God is glorious in His creation, and creation is holy because of God.

We must never create dichotomies where they do not exist. Least of all, should we separate the Creator from His creation. The two belong together because that is how God has chosen to reveal Himself to us. "The heavens declare the glory of God, and the firmament proclaims his handiwork" (Ps 19:2).

3. **Let us proclaim the mystery of faith.** (Eucharistic Prayer, the Proclamation of Faith)

> *Undeniably great is the mystery of devotion,*
> *Who was manifested in the flesh,*
> *vindicated in the spirit,*
> *seen by angels,*
> *proclaimed to the Gentiles,*
> *believed in throughout the world,*
> *taken up in glory.* (1 Tm 3:16)

"Let us proclaim the mystery of faith," exhorts the priest. Notice that he does not say, "Let us proclaim *a* mystery of faith," but *the* mystery. And what is that mystery? It is the mystery of the Lord's passion, death, and resurrection sacramentally re-enacted upon the altar, bringing the central event of human history into the present. It is the mystery of the incarnation extended in space and time through the Church. It is the mystery of God's love for humanity, the sign of His desire to be close to those He loves. It is the mystery which looks to the day of Christ's return as Judge of the world, ushering in those days when sacraments shall cease because God "will be all in all."

And all this explains why we fast, why we genuflect, why we receive Holy Communion only in the state of grace, why we have a special love for the priests who bring us this mystery, and why we are concerned with fostering vocations in young men to take their places.

Yes, we behold *the* mystery, before which we kneel in humble adoration.

4. Pray, brethren, that our sacrifice may be acceptable to God, the almighty Father. (Liturgy of the Eucharist, Prayer over the Gifts)

> *For from the rising of the sun, even to its setting,*
>   *my name is great among the nations;*
> *And everywhere they bring sacrifice to my name,*
>   *and a pure offering.* (Mal 1:11)

"Pray, brethren, that our sacrifice may be acceptable to God the almighty Father," the priest urges.

Each time you participate in the celebration of the Mass you fulfill the prophecy of Malachi, for the Sacrifice of the Mass is the fulfillment and culmination of every Old Testament sacrifice because of its victim and its participants.

Under the Old Covenant, animals were sacrificed who stood in the worshipers' stead. On Calvary, Jesus the Son of God Himself stood in our stead. He offered Himself as a ransom for the many:

> Then he took a cup, gave thanks, and gave it to them, and they all drank from it. He said to them: "This is my blood of the covenant, which will be shed for many." (Mk 14:23-24)

At Mass this once-for-all act of Christ the High Priest is represented for us in order to bring to mind the effects of His sacrificial death and to call down the blessings of salvation wrought by that sacrifice on us, who are now present:

> It was fitting that we should have a high priest: holy, innocent, undefiled, separated from sinners, higher than the heavens. He has no need, as did the high priests, to offer sacrifice day after day, first for his own sins and then for those of the people; he did that once for all when he offered himself. (Heb 7:26-27)

The sacrifices of the Old Testament were offered only by Jews and thus benefitted only the Jews. The sacrifice of the New Covenant is offered by the Church throughout the world, and the body of Christ broken for our sins—which reunited humanity to God on Calvary—now takes on an added dimension. It still unites us to God but also unites each of us to one another as common sharers in the Body and Blood of the victim offered to God and returned to us as our food and pledge of everlasting life: "I am the living bread that came down from heaven; whoever eats this bread will live forever; and the bread that I will give is my flesh for the life of the world" (Jn 6:51).

In offering the Mass, we give to God the greatest gift possible. He sees His obedient and loving Son pleading for us and is moved to mercy. If we learn anything from the Mass, let it be to become obedient and loving children of God like Jesus and to strive to be merciful like the Father.

Thus we will most surely fulfill this prophecy; lives lived in this manner will make the name of the Lord "great among the nations" because they will be reflections of the life of Christ.

5. **You formed man in your own likeness**
   and set him over the whole world
   to serve you, his creator,
   and to rule over all creatures.
   Even when he disobeyed you and lost your
   friendship
   you did not abandon him to the power of
   death, ... (Eucharistic Prayer IV)

The serpent said to the woman: "You certainly will not die! No, God knows well that the moment you eat of it your eyes will be opened and you will be like gods who know what is good and what is bad." (Gn 3:4-5)

In the midst of a beautiful relationship of love, tragedy strikes—man and woman want to go it alone. From our very beginnings we have resisted God's promptings to live a life in communion with God Himself and our fellows. In the Genesis account, humanity is presented with the perennial temptation to be a god—in the wrong sense—to be self-sufficient and autonomous.

It is important to take note of the fact that God Himself is a Community, a plurality of Persons, a Trinity. To strive to be god-like was not a sin for our first parents, but the desire to do it on their own was. Or maybe they thought that divinity was something to which they were entitled. Even the Son of God did not cling to what was rightfully His but became a man like us, in all things but sin.

To aspire to divinity is the noblest of human yearnings. It is implanted in us by God Himself to keep us on the road back to Him. That is why we should reflect very carefully on the words we pray each day at Mass: "... may we come to share in the divinity of Christ who humbled himself to share in our humanity."

We need to look to the example of Jesus the Perfect Man, the Second Adam, who brought us the possibility of becoming gods—the right way—by submission to the will of the Father, by service of one's fellows, by forgetfulness of self. Yes, we can become gods with a small "g," for perfect humanity leads to divinity. Christ is our example, our promise, and our assurance.

6. Do this in memory of me. (Eucharistic Prayer)

You shall observe this as a perpetual ordinance for yourselves and your descendants. (Ex 12:24)

God is asking the Israelites to recall the Passover as "a perpetual ordinance." Of all the commandments God gave the Israelites, this may have been the most important, for it asks that they remember Him and their salvation forever.

Likewise, of all Jesus' requests, none was so crucial as this same command, in the context of that same meal of the covenant, the Passover: "Then he took the bread, said the blessing, broke it, and gave it to them, saying, "This is my body, which will be given for you; do this in memory of me" (Lk 22:19). And what was this meal by which we are to remember Him, but the holy Eucharist?

Why do we honor the Eucharist with incense, candles, bells, hymns, a sanctuary lamp, and genuflections? For one reason and one reason alone: Because God has come into our midst. Our memory of His love and saving deeds is so strong that at the word of remembrance, the Word of God once more descends to earth to be with us. As St. Thomas Aquinas put it so beautifully in his *Pange Lingue*, "By a word the Word embodied changes common bread and wine."

We Christians have failed our Savior in many ways, but we must never fail to remember Him in the Eucharist because it is there that we hear His Word of love proclaimed and receive the proof of that love as food. And when we remember the Lord, we must remember what He did for all people; and, therefore, what He wants us to do for them.

If we forget the eucharistic Christ, we have forgotten what it means to be Christian. We will no longer be able to be Christians because we will no longer hear His words of love and receive His Body and Blood given up for us.

"Come, Lord Jesus" (Rv 22:20).

7. **Father, it is our duty and our salvation,**
   always and everywhere
   to give you thanks
   through your beloved Son, Jesus Christ.
   (Eucharistic Prayer II)

> *"In the meeting tent, outside the veil that hangs in front of the commandments, Aaron shall set up the lamps to burn before the LORD regularly, from evening till morning. Thus, by a perpetual statute for you and your descendants, the lamps shall be set up on the pure gold lampstand, to burn regularly before the LORD."* (Lv 24:3-4)

Isn't it unfortunate that once we get used to something, we take it for granted? Once we know the meaning of a symbol, its significance gradually fades. Just the opposite should be true. We should learn even more from the symbol the longer it is with us. We modern Catholics must rediscover our symbols and appreciate them, as if for the first time. They should nurture our faith and inspire us.

One such symbol is the lamp burning in our sanctuaries. That lamp is a sign of the eucharistic presence and perpetual love of God in our midst. That is why God commanded the Israelites that it remain ever-lit. The Christian sanctuary lamp is a reminder which says:

Jesus is always here; He is here because He loves you. The Christian sanctuary lamp is an invitation: To love and thank Him in return; to follow the example of the lamp which burns itself out for God. The Christian sanctuary lamp is a challenge: To love others as God has loved us.

Questions for Group Discussion

1. In speaking of the Eucharist, why is it best to describe the altar as an altar in its own right, rather than a table?

2. Describe the basic structure of the Eucharistic Prayer. Discuss each part and its significance.

3. To whom is the Eucharistic Prayer addressed? Why? What are the implications?

4. What is the relationship between Christ's once-for-all death on the cross and what is done in the Mass?

5. How does sacred memory lead to sacred reality in the liturgy? Discuss.

CHAPTER FOUR

RECEIVING THE LORD AND CALLED FORTH TO SERVE: COMMUNION AND CONCLUDING RITES

Receiving the Lord and Called Forth to Serve: Communion and Concluding Rites

T HE ENGLISH WORD "Communion" has its roots in the Greek *koinonia*, which includes notions of fellowship, unity, sharing, and community. With whom does a believer have communion? First of all, with the Lord, and from that essential unity comes union with all other believers. In other words, if the vertical relationship is in order, it overflows into a wholesome horizontal relationship.

The Communion Rite of the Mass begins with the Lord's Prayer, which deals with both the vertical and horizontal dimensions of communion. That is the very reason for its inclusion in the rite. The prayer begins with the pure praise of God and then moves on to more earthly concerns, as well as the expression of a desire to be as merciful as God Himself.

The Latin introduction puts it all very clearly: "Taught by our Savior's command and formed by the Word of God, we dare to say. . . ." The English translation most often used, however, fails to capture the critical points: a) We pray in these words, in obedience to the directives of Christ; b) the words we use are His very own; c) to call God "Father" would be an outrageous and nearly blasphemous act, were we not empowered to do so by the command and indeed the grace of Christ, by which we become adopted sons and daughters of God.

THE LORD'S PRAYER

Without embarking on a detailed exegesis of the Lord's Prayer, it might still be helpful to provide some analysis. Jesus' relationship with the Father was unique, enabling Him to speak to God in the most intimate manner—not simply as "Father" but as "Daddy." On our own "steam"—even as creatures of God, we cannot address Him in this manner. It is only in and through the redemption wrought by Christ that we can properly and without fear approach God in these terms.

Without Christ, we are what St. Paul so properly called us: "Children of wrath" (Eph 2:3). This concept is not too popular today. Pop psychology tells us, "I'm okay, you're okay." But the truth of the matter is that without Christ, no one is "okay"—and the value of Christianity rises and falls on that very point. That is why the human race was sent the Son of God. That is why He redeemed us. That is why He established a

Church, and that is the only reason we celebrate the Eucharist. Hence, the importance of having this understanding in mind before approaching the altar. Any lesser notion will rob the Eucharist of its saving power.

As the prayer continues, we ask that the Lord's Name be revered and that His "will be done on earth as it is in heaven." When is God's Name "hallowed" or reverenced? When human beings do His will, just as Jesus did, which is the essence of the Eucharistic Sacrifice now become our food. And so, we petition: "Give us this day our daily bread." We ask not only for physical nourishment but, far more importantly, for "the Bread of Life," Who is Christ Himself.

The history of world religions demonstrates that worshipers could participate most fully in the sacrifice offered by taking a portion of that sacrifice. It is only at this moment in the liturgical celebration, then, that one can correctly and with theological accuracy refer to the Eucharist as food, a banquet, a meal. A unique significance has been conferred on the meal, precisely because it is the sacrifice of Christ.

Having expressed a desire to receive Christ, one must live out the implications of that action. Therefore, wce plead for the ability to forgive others as God has forgiven us in Christ. Last of all, we pray for the necessary grace to respond to the temptations of the Evil One with the same resoluteness of our brother and Lord, Who banished Satan from His presence, rather than disregard the Father's plan for His life:

Then the devil took him up to a very high mountain, and showed him all the kingdoms of the world in their magnificence, and he said to him, "All these I shall give you, if you will prostrate yourself and worship me." At this, Jesus said to him, "Get away, Satan!"

It is written:

"The Lord, your God, shall you worship and him alone shall you serve." (Mt 4:8-10)

Praying in the words of Jesus means putting on the mind and heart of Christ, and this permits us to continue in our journey toward the consummation or climax of the rite in Holy Communion. The priest picks up on the petition for deliverance from evil in the prayer known as the *embolism*. The stress is on a desire to be free from sin as fitting preparation for two comings of Christ—imminently in the Eucharist and then at the end of time, the *eschaton*. The Eucharist is rightly described as an eschatological banquet for this very reason—it prepares the Church to greet her bridegroom when He comes in glory.

The people's response is the so-called "Protestant ending" to the Lord's Prayer, about which a few clarifications are in order. The acclamation antedates Protestantism by a dozen centuries at least. It seems that an Eastern monk was copying the Scriptures. When he got to the Lord's Prayer, he was moved to a personal hymn of praise (doxology), which he wrote into the margin of the text. Gradually, it was tacked onto the Our Father in the Eastern Churches and subsequently taken over by the Protestant Reformers.

The Church of the West resisted its use in conjunction with the Lord's Prayer not because it is heretical (clearly it is not), but simply because it is inaccurate to include at the beginning—inasmuch as it does not contain the words "taught by our Savior's command." The doxology's inclusion at this point, however, is a good way to join the present and the eschatological elements of the Eucharist in such a way that our focus can be directed to the building up of God's kingdom here on earth and to its fulfillment at the *parousia* ("the second coming").

SIGN OF PEACE

The prayer for peace harks back to the risen Lord's conferral of "shalom" on His terrified band of apostles on Easter night. Since it is God's own peace and not the world's, we can be confident of a true and lasting experience of it. The priest utters a beautiful line glossed over all too quickly at times: "Look not on our sins, but on the faith of your Church. . . ."

At this moment, gazing upon the spotless Lamb of God before him on the altar, the priest becomes painfully aware of his own sinfulness and that of his people, and thus does the only sensible thing. He asks the Lord to ignore our individual sinfulness and instead to regard the sinlessness of the whole Church. In essence, we seek refuge in the community which has already been cleansed by the Blood of the Lamb—a powerful reminder of exactly what membership in Christ's Church signifies.

The priest then extends a wish that this peace of Christ be with each and every member of the assembly. He or the deacon may also invite everyone to share "the peace" with each other. Actually, we have here more than a mere wish. It is far more a declaration of the peace that does indeed exist between the people and God and among themselves.

Ironically, the Sign of Peace has been one of the major sources of conflict in the revised liturgy, and so a number of points might be made at this juncture. First, the rite is entirely optional—to be done at the celebrant's discretion. Therefore, some priests use it all the time; some never do; some only on Sundays; yet others omit it for Advent or Lent.

Second, the Sign of Peace has been a part of the Mass from the earliest days. By the Middle Ages, however, it was generally restricted to the ministers of the Mass in the sanctuary, and the gesture was a sacred embrace.

Third, the extension of the gesture to the entire congregation has raised some questions about its potentially disruptive influence at a particularly solemn time, leading some liturgists to call for its transfer to the beginning of the liturgy or to the Offertory. This latter option is employed in the Anglican liturgy as the priest recalls the Lord's injunction to make peace with one's brother before offering one's gift at the altar:

"If you bring your gift to the altar, and there recall that your brother has anything against you, leave your gift there at the altar, go first and be reconciled with your brother, and then come and offer your gift." (Mt 5:23-24)

Fourth, some objections deal with the emptiness of a handshake for so profound a reality as the shared experience of God's peace for all eternity.

Regardless of how the issue is eventually resolved by the Church, in the interim the Sign of Peace certainly should not be a divisive element nor an occasion to upset the steady and solemn progress of the liturgy toward its final goal.

Next is recited or sung the Lamb of God, which echoes the words of John the Baptist when first he announced the identity of Jesus to the world:

The next day he saw Jesus coming toward him and said, "Behold, the Lamb of God, who takes away the sin of the world. He is the one of whom I said, 'A man is coming after me who ranks ahead of me because he existed before me.'" (Jn 1:29-30)

COMMUNION

While the Lamb's litany is being prayed, the celebrant breaks the sacred Host, ideally allowing for at least some of the people to receive particles from the same Host as he, in order to underscore the unity of the sacrament. A small particle of the Lord's Body is then dropped into the chalice, symbolizing the re-uniting of

His Body and Blood, which is to say, His resurrection. The bread and wine are consecrated separately to signify the death of the Lord, but in Holy Communion we receive not the dead Christ but the risen Lord.

The priest prays quietly one of two prayers as his private preparation for Holy Communion. Then, raising the sacred Host aloft, he repeats once more the words of John the Baptist and invites all those properly disposed to come forward. The Latin original speaks of the blessedness of "those who are called to the wedding feast of the Lamb"—a lovely allusion to the Lamb of God and the marriage of Christ and His Church spoken of in the Book of Revelation:

> Then the angel said to me, "Write this: Blessed are those who have been called to the wedding feast of the Lamb." And he said to me, "These words are true; they come from God." (Rv 19:9)

The congregation responds with an admission of their own unworthiness to receive Christ, in imitation of the Roman centurion who sought healing for his servant. The English translation does not make this connection as clear as it could be, while the Latin quotes the centurion directly: "I am not worthy that you should come under my roof, but only say the word and my soul (servant) shall be healed" (Mt 8:8).

What does it mean to be "properly disposed" or "worthy" to receive our Lord in Holy Communion? Three things are required: incorporation into Christ's Church through Baptism; being in the state of grace;

observing the law of fast (one hour for liquid and solid food alike, unless impeded from doing so because of sickness—water does not break the fast), so as to demonstrate and even feel a genuine "hunger" for the Bread of Life.

The first two issues call for some special consideration. In these days of ecumenical dialogue and activity, frequently people ask: When may a Protestant or Orthodox believer receive Holy Communion in the Roman Catholic Church? They may do so under the most restricted circumstances: The Christian in question must not have access to his or her own minister for a prolonged period of time and should be in a situation of grave spiritual need (for instance, a time of religious persecution). That same person must profess the same eucharistic faith as the Roman Catholic Church. He or she must also request Communion on his or her own initiative.

As should be obvious, these conditions would be rather hard to verify in the United States. Does the Church hold to this to be mean-spirited? Not at all, for something extremely fundamental is at stake here.

Indiscriminate intercommunion undermines both the Eucharist and the Church. Catholics see a deep relationship between eucharistic communion and ecclesial communion. It is not an accident that the names of the Bishop of Rome and the local bishop are mentioned in the Eucharistic Prayer. This recalls the fact that any who would *receive* Communion must *be* in communion with those two successors of the apostles, precisely because it is through union with them and under their authority that the Eucharist is effected. Thus one must already be in full communion with the holy Roman Catholic Church as the body of Christ, in order to receive the Body of Christ in the Eucharist.

Some argue that intercommunion will hasten the day of Christian unity, but this assertion does not correspond to reality. Denominations that practice intercommunion are no closer to one another today than when they started. Just ask Episcopalians and Old Catholics. All too often, they become sloppy in their efforts at dialogue, precisely because they have "jumped the gun." Four centuries of disunity cannot be undone in the twinkling of an eye.

Under similar conditions, can Catholics receive from Orthodox or Protestant clergy? That would only be possible if the minister were validly ordained; otherwise, he would not be able to confect (consecrate) the Eucharist—no valid priesthood, no valid Eucharist. For the most part, that would mean that Catholic reception of Communion could only occur through the ministrations of Eastern Orthodox priests. However, it should be noted that, in general, the Orthodox hold to an even stricter discipline on this than we. Therefore, we would not be welcome to receive Holy Communion from them, even were our own law to permit it.

Not receiving Communion can, at times, be an excellent form of penance offered for the success of the ecumenical movement. For example, I always encourage Orthodox and Protestants present at Mass (especially for occasions like weddings and funerals) to use Communion time to pray for Christian unity, so that

Christ's will that his Church be one will become a reality. I would encourage Catholics to do the same when attending a Protestant wedding or funeral. Tolerating anything less than the full reality does a disservice to the cause of unity and the integrity of the Eucharist.

What about being in the state of grace? Very simply, that means not being conscious of having committed grave sin since one's last sacramental confession. While it is not necessary to receive the Sacrament of Penance before each reception of Holy Communion, it is required to do so if one has sinned grievously, lest one make a sacrilegious Communion. St. Paul warns about this in the strongest of terms:

> Whoever eats the bread and drinks the cup of the Lord unworthily will have to answer for the body and blood of the Lord. A person should examine himself, and so eat the bread and drink the cup. For anyone who eats and drinks without discerning the body, eats and drinks judgment on himself.
>
> (1 Cor 11:27-29)

Yet this apostolic admonition is widely ignored in many instances. The Greek liturgy has the priest declare "Hagia Hagiois" ("Holy things for the holy"), thus emphasizing the need for those receiving the Eucharist to be as blameless as possible for this saving encounter. .

Communicants approach the altar in procession. They are accompanied by the singing of an appropriate eucharistic hymn or recitation of the Communion antiphon. The procession and singing symbolize the movement of God's people toward their final goal, Who is Christ.

The ordinary ministers of Holy Communion to the faithful are to be in Sacred Orders—that is, bishops, priests, or deacons. In extraordinary circumstances, lay people or religious who have been commissioned by the bishop as extraordinary ministers of Holy Communion may assist the ordinary ministers. Such circumstances would be the lack of an ordinary minister, the inability of an ordinary minister to distribute Communion because of illness or advanced age, or an unwieldy number of communicants with an insufficient number of ordinary ministers.

To let the use of extraordinary ministers prevail on a regular or normal basis without such circumstances is a serious abuse, sadly all too common in certain places, and described by Pope John Paul II as a "reprehensible" practice.

Communicants may receive either standing or kneeling. If they stand, they should either bow or genuflect beforehand as a profession of faith in the Real Presence of Christ in the Eucharist and as an act of adoration.

Universal liturgical law mandates the reception of Holy Communion on the tongue, although certain countries have received an indult (special permission) from the Holy See for Communion to be received on the hand. If the option legitimately exists, a communicant may never be forced to receive on the hand.

The Churches of the East permit neither extraordinary ministers of Holy Communion nor Communion on the hand.

In the early Church, Holy Communion was usually administered under the forms of both bread and wine. For a variety of reasons, Communion of the faithful gradually came to be restricted to the form of bread alone.

The Protestant Reformers latched onto this issue and argued that sacramental validity depended upon reception under both species. The Church at the Council of Trent responded by reminding all that the Lord is fully present under either form. Therefore, those who receive only under the form of bread receive the whole Christ, as would one who receives only under the form of wine. For example, a sick person may be unable to consume solid food, or an alcoholic may find it unwise to receive Communion under the form of wine. To deal with the doctrinal question in a definitive manner, Trent insisted on Communion under one species alone for the Church of the West, while the churches of the East maintained their ancient tradition of both species by intinction. In this procedure, the priest dips the consecrated Bread into the precious Blood and then places it into the mouth of the communicant.

Since Vatican II the church has permitted Holy Communion under both forms for certain occasions, since there is no longer any attack on sacramental validity for the use of only one species. If the faithful are to receive under the form of wine, two options exist:

intinction (which then rules out Communion in the hand, for obvious reasons) or direct reception from the chalice. If the second option is employed, the celebrant must see to it that the sacred Species are handled carefully, so as to avoid spilling. Furthermore, this should never be the pretext for using extraordinary ministers of Holy Communion, as Cardinal Joseph Ratzinger of the Congregation for the Doctrine of the Faith has stressed.

The Church guards the Eucharist jealously because it is her most precious possession. The various regulations are designed to highlight this fact. After all, how we treat the Eucharist indicates what we think of it. Little would be accomplished by verbally professing our belief in the Real Presence if our actions belied it. And so, the Church's concern for external signs of reverence and devotion is understandable.

The sacred vessels are purified at a side table or at the side of the altar by the celebrant or deacon, after which all sit for a period of reflection and thanksgiving for the great gift the Father has bestowed upon us. Those sentiments are vocalized in the Prayer after Communion, which brings to a conclusion the Communion Rite.

THE CONCLUDING RITE

If any announcements are necessary, they are made now and should be brief, lest it appear that a second homily is being given. Some parishes make the announcements before the liturgy even begins. In reality, if the people are trained to take home and read the parish bulletin, "commercial interruptions" should be able to be minimized.

The dramatic action falls quickly now as the priest extends the final greeting and blessing. The opening words of the Mass, for the Lord's grace and peace to be with all, and the opening act of the sign of the cross likewise form the Concluding Rites. The assembly is dismissed by the deacon or priest. The celebrant kisses the altar, genuflects to the Blessed Sacrament, and leaves with the other ministers as the choir and/or congregation sing the recessional hymn.

It is worth noting a sentence in Latin for the Rite of Dismissal: "Ite, missa est." Literally, that means, "Go, it (the Church or congregation) has been sent." "Missa" (dismissal) gradually and eventually became the name for the entire service. That translates into English as "Mass." This is surely a proper designation, too, because it emphasizes the on-going nature of the Mass in our daily lives. True believers do not leave their religious commitment within the four walls of the church building for the limited span of forty-five to sixty minutes on a Sunday. Rather, the deepest meaning of the Eucharist requires one to represent Christ and His Gospel in all the circumstances of one's life: at home, in school, at work, in public life. Failure to do so is an ignorance of or a refusal to be for others the Body of Christ that one has received—and that is the heart of the Christian vocation.

SCRIPTURAL MEDITATIONS FOR
THE COMMUNION AND CONCLUDING RITES

1. The body of Christ. (Communion Rite)

I will now rain down bread from heaven for you. Each day the people are to go out and gather their daily portion.
(Ex 16:4)

How wonderful is God's Providence! In the Hebrews' journey to the Promised Land, the Lord gave them "bread from heaven." In our journey back to God, we Christians are fed with "bread from heaven." Yet more marvelous and efficacious than the manna, this Bread is not merely physical sustenance; it is the very Body of Christ given to be our strength and consolation as we pass through the desert to the Promised Land.

In the Eucharist we receive the Lord as individual persons, but also as members of a community. Like the Israelites, we do not stand alone before God. The Church, the new Israel, comes before the Father as the people whom Christ has purchased by His saving death. If we are part of this community, what are our obligations to it?

We must have the same attitude as God Himself. What moved Him to feed this community with heavenly bread? Love, compassion, mercy, forgiveness. If our sentiments are not the same, we betray the table fellowship we share; we deny the reality which God is trying to convey: The unity and equality of all who receive the one Bread.

It is sad that many Christians today do not realize the tremendous gift they have in the Eucharist. They "get nothing out of it." It was just such people who left Jesus when He spoke of eating His Body and Blood: "Then many of His disciples who were listening said, 'This saying is hard; who can accept it?' " (Jn 6:60). Jesus then asked His inner circle of disciples if they would also leave Him. But Peter did accept the Lord's saying and replied in the manner we must emulate: "Master, to whom shall we go? You have the words of eternal life" (Jn 6:68).

2. For the kingdom, the power, and the glory are yours, now and forever. (Communion Rite)

All the angels stood around the throne and around the elders and the four living creatures. They prostrated themselves before the throne, worshiped God, and exclaimed:

"Amen. Blessing and glory, wisdom and thanksgiving,
honor, power, and might
be to our God forever and ever. Amen."

(Rv 7:11-12)

What an awesome reality is expressed here as the angels and saints reverence the Lord God in the heavenly liturgy—acknowledging that all honor, power, and glory belongs to Him forever and ever! Just so, we acknowledge the kingship and sovereignty of God in this age and forever in the liturgy where our worship—in a very real sense—is joined to that of heaven. Such a spirit of reverence and praise should always characterize our worship of Almighty God, especially in the liturgy when we are allowed to enter into heavenly places and join the worship of the saints and angels.

Sadly, many approach the holy Sacrifice of the Mass with a casual, if not impatient attitude. They do not fathom the sacred mysteries and treat them as simply something to be "gotten through" on Sunday morning. Their real focus is on the leisure activities they want to pursue after Sunday Mass.

But men and women were not made simply to pursue their own pleasure; they were made for the glory and worship of God in heaven forever. In the Sacrifice of the Mass, we have the unique opportunity to enter into that heavenly worship. This is the worship of the Lord God before which prophets of old and mighty kings trembled in holy fear and anticipation. This great act of worship reaches a high point in the Rite of Communion as we prepare to receive the Lamb of God Who sits upon the throne. This is the Lamb Who is reverenced and adored by myriads of angels and the saints and martyrs dressed in festal garments.

Let us behold the sacred mysteries of which we partake and reverence Almighty God in spirit and truth, for He is worthy of our worship now and forever.

3. Lord, may I receive these gifts in purity of heart. May they bring me healing and strength, now and for ever. (Communion Rite, prayer of the priest while purifying the chalice and the paten after Communion)

> *"The whole priestly tribe of Levi shall have no share in the heritage with Israel; they shall live on the oblations of the* LORD *and the portions due to him. Levi shall have no heritage among his brothers; the* LORD *himself is his heritage, as he has told him."* (Dt 18:1-2)

Christian priests inherit the priesthood of the Old Covenant but have as their very special model Jesus the eternal High Priest, Who most certainly has the Lord God for His heritage. Every Christian must have the Lord for his heritage but most especially the priest, for he stands with the rest of the people yet presumes to go beyond and approach the Father for them.

His dedication to Almighty God must be total. That means that he does no work but that of Christ. He has no family but the Church. He knows no joy greater than his service of the Lord. His must be an undivided attention to the things of God for the salvation of humanity.

And while the world of the priesthood is joyful, awe-inspiring, and beautiful, there are also days when it is frustrating, unclear, and dissatisfying because of our weak human nature and the intangible realities with which they deal.

Therefore, love your priests. Seek to understand

your priests. Be grateful to your priests, most particularly for being instruments by which the eucharistic Christ comes among us. Finally, persevere in praying for your priests, in the hope that they will continue to lead you to God.

4. This is the Lamb of God who takes away the sins of the world. (Communion Rite)

"Take this scroll of the law and put it beside the ark of the covenant of the LORD, your God, that there it may be a witness against you." (Dt 31:26)

As we move from the Old Testament to the New Testament, we cannot help but notice a pattern of fulfillment. We see the same symbol evolve to its greatest significance. The Ark of the Covenant went through just such a transition. The ark contained the heart of the Jewish faith: the law. Our ark, the tabernacle, also contains the heart of our faith: the eucharistic Christ, the Lamb of God upon the Mercy Seat, Who pleads for us.

And what a wondrous fulfillment has occurred—from the Law to the Person of Christ. Christians are freed from the Law, says St. Paul: "Now we are released from the law, dead to what held us captive, so that we may serve in the newness of the spirit and not under the obsolete letter" (Rom 7:6). Clearly, Paul does not mean absolute license. On the contrary, it is very challenging because it means fidelity—to a person. So Jesus has freed us from a slavery to the Law but has called us to show forth our love by responding generously and freely.

We should also note another change: The Law is seen as a "witness against" the sinner. How fortunate that Jesus has replaced it, for He is not a "witness against" us but a mediator and faithful intercessor on our behalf with His heavenly Father:

> To that same degree has Jesus [also] become the guarantee of an [even] better covenant. Those priests were many because they were prevented by death from remaining in office, but he, because he remains forever, has a priesthood that does not pass away. Therefore he is always able to save those who approach God through him, since he lives forever to make intercession for them. (Heb 7:22-25)

And so, the next time you genuflect before our ark of the covenant to worship the Lamb, reflect on the change that has occurred. From the heart, thank God for such a marvelous replacement as His own divine Son.

5. Bow your heads and pray for God's blessing. (Concluding Rite)

> *The Lord said to Abram: "Go forth from the land of your kinsfolk and from your father's house to a land that I will show you.*
>
> *"I will make of you a great nation,*
> *and I will bless you;*

> *I will make your name great,*
>   *so that you will be a blessing.*
> *I will bless those that bless you*
>   *and curse those who curse you.*
> *All the communities of the earth*
>   *shall find blessing in you."* (Gn 12:1-3)

Prejudice . . . poverty . . . corruption . . . immorality. Are not these a substantial part of the reality of modern life? Even of "good Christians"? Yet God promised Abraham thousands of years ago that his descendants would serve as a blessing for the whole earth. We who worship the God of Abraham and Jesus must be living blessings to this world of ours, or else we impede the coming of His kingdom, which is the fulfillment of the covenant.

If the Lord could give such an utterly marvelous assurance at the dawn of the emergence of the chosen people, what greater things can occur through us, his people living in the fullness of time? We have the benefit of millennia of revelation, the life of Jesus, the lived experience of two thousand years as the Lord's body, His Church. But have Christians been the blessing they can be?

G. K. Chesterton once put it very well: "It is not that Christianity has been tried and found wanting; it has been found hard and not tried." This should not make us despondent or pessimistic because each age has raised up its own saints to be that "blessing." This must serve as a challenge. Our actions should be a reflection of our faith, so that others see what Christianity is all about.

With the Eucharist as your strength, act as if you are the saint this generation needs. You are!

6. **Go in peace to love and serve the Lord.** (Concluding Rite)

"Israel shall make a sanctuary for me, that I may dwell in their midst. This Dwelling and all its furnishings you shall make exactly according to the pattern that I will now show you." (Ex 25:8-9)

A recent trend which is rather disturbing is a subtle appeal to contradict this passage of Scripture and others like it. The trend is one which denies the value of building churches—or at least beautiful ones. Sometimes those who advocate this position go so far as to say that it is against the spirit of the Gospel. Nothing could be further from the truth.

Throughout Scripture we find God asking that a place of worship be built for him. Our Lord Himself went to the synagogue and Temple. People who berate churches do not understand their function. A church is meant to be a place for encountering Almighty God in a unique manner. It is supposed to be a beautiful place whose atmosphere inspires. A church should be an oasis of peace and comfort for people whose lives are all too often scenes of strife, suffering, and conflict.

Even some very well-intentioned people fall into this

trap, but they need to recall that Jesus accepted the extravagant anointing of Mary Magdalene and praised her for it:

> ... "Why do you make trouble for [the] woman? She has done a good thing for me. The poor you will always have with you; but you will not always have me. In pouring this perfumed oil upon my body, she did it to prepare me for burial." (Mt 26:10-12)

The one who murmured against this deed was Judas.

Therefore, let us continue to build majestic sanctuaries, so that God may continue to dwell among us. Let the eucharistic Christ Who is the sign of that presence motivate us to go from the house of God to the house of men with the joyous news of love we have received and now wish to share. In the words of the priest at the conclusion of the Mass, "Go in peace to love and serve the Lord."

7. Thanks be to God. (Concluding Rite)

> *Happy the man who ..., delights in the law of the LORD and meditates on his law day and night.* (Ps 1:1-2)

> *Let everything that has breath praise the LORD! Alleuia.* (Ps 150:6)

The Psalter begins in praise of God's Law; it ends by inviting all creation to join in that act of adoration. And rightly so.

If the individual believer commits himself to a life of

obedience to his Creator, that person experiences harmony in life. That means peace within oneself, peace with one's God, peace with one's brothers and sisters in the human family, and peace with all the rest of God's creatures. The lesson of Genesis is that sin begets discord, while holiness and righteousness beget that state best described by the Hebrew word *shalom*— that peace, harmony, and inner wholeness which is God's gift for those who obey His Law.

In his last outpouring of praise to the Lord, the psalmist joyously invites "everything that has breath" to join in the concert. Man and woman reconciled with God reconcile, in turn, the whole of creation.

That is the whole point of the covenant renewal ceremony known as the Eucharistic Sacrifice. And what is our response? Let us go forth from Mass, saying and truly meaning, "Thanks be to God."

Questions for Group Discussion

1. What makes the Lord's Prayer a proper beginning for the Communion Rite?

2. What is meant by referring to the Mass as an "eschatalogical banquet"? See Revelation 19:9. Discuss.

3. With whom does a believer enjoy fellowship after receiving Holy Communion?

4. Note several signs of special reverence that are shown to the Blessed Sacrament during the Communion Rite. Why are these external signs important? Discuss.

5. What does the Church expect of one who has received Holy Communion? How does the Concluding Rite reflect that expectation?

Appendices

Latin in the Liturgy

I N LIGHT OF THE SCHISM of Archbishop Marcel Lefebvre and his followers, it might be well to consider the place of Latin in the Church's liturgy. In reality, the dispute between the Holy See and the excommunicated prelate has nothing to do with the use of Latin. Unfortunately, though, that is the way in which the issue is generally perceived. Thus, it becomes the "hook" used to attract unsuspecting people into the movement.

Reflect on the following citations:

The use of the Latin language ... is to be preserved in the Latin rites. (*Sacrosanctum Concilium*, n. 36)

... care must be taken to ensure that the faithful may also be able to say or sing together in Latin those parts of the Ordinary of the Mass which pertain to them. (*Sacrosanctum Concilium*, n. 54)

The Church recognizes Gregorian Chant as being specially suited to the Roman liturgy. Therefore, other things being equal, it should be given pride of place in liturgical services. (*Sacrosanctum Concilium*, n. 116)

All of the above passages come from the Vatican II Constitution on the Sacred Liturgy. Yet so many people, including otherwise well-informed Catholics, labor under the impression that the Council banished Latin from the Church's worship life. As can be readily seen, the opposite is really the case. It is the vernacular which requires permission, not Latin. Why would the Council Fathers have been so strong in their support of Latin?

A sacral language underscores the uniqueness of the event being celebrated. Therefore, in almost every major world religion, a special language was reserved for worship. The Jews of our Lord's day spoke Aramaic but continued to use Hebrew for worship. Those of the Eastern Rites of the Catholic Church, who always prayed in the vernacular, nonetheless use a somewhat archaic form of the particular language for the liturgy. Even the Anglican Communion's Book of Common Prayer, before its recent revision, and the King James Bible do not correspond to the English of the street.

Indeed, there seems to be within the human person an innate desire to keep something for God alone. This insight was brought home to me many years ago in a conversation with a charismatic Catholic. The man told me that speaking in tongues had the advantage of enabling him to worship Almighty God in a language in which he had never cursed another man.

One may logically ask just what Latin has to offer Catholics living at the close of the twentieth century.

First, it links a particular gathering of God's people to generations of believers who have worshiped in those very words for centuries and to all the other Catholic faithful around the globe.

Second, in a shrinking world, Latin is a vehicle for unity. Its pre-Vatican II opponents often remarked snidely that the great "advantage" of Latin was that one could go to Mass anywhere in the world and know what was being said. However, today travelers have even greater difficulty understanding a Mass offered in a totally foreign tongue. The Latin liturgy in large population centers is a sign of Christian hospitality and a confirmation of our unity.

Third, in the Vatican or at major shrines, Latin allows our unity to shine through in a unique manner. Imagine the power of hearing the Profession of Faith sung in St. Peter's Square by a quarter of a million believers from every nation on earth. It is nothing less than the fulfillment of the Pentecost Preface which prays for the grace to proclaim one faith with one voice.

Pope Pius XII once declared that the day the Church abandoned Latin, she would be driven back into the catacombs. By that he meant that her ability to worship as a unified body would be seriously hampered.

That insight struck home on a pilgrimage to Medjugorje. At times the shrine staff directed people to recite prayers in their own languages simultaneously. It sounded like a contemporary Tower of Babel. In other situations, they indicated that certain hymns or parts of the Mass should be sung in Latin, but many (including priests, especially Americans) were incapable of doing so because they had forgotten the Latin words or had never been taught them to begin with.

Obviously, Catholics cannot use Latin for international gatherings if they never do so at other times. A modest proposal would be to begin using Pope Paul VI's *Jubilante Deo*. This booklet of Gregorian chants was issued by the pontiff in the years after the Council as he became alarmed at the gradual demise of Latin. Included here are familiar and simple melodies for the *Kyrie, Gloria, Credo, Sanctus, Agnus Dei*, and several hymns.

What are the options open for Latin in the Church's liturgy today? I see three broad categories.

First, the Mass in Latin according to the revised rites of Pope Paul VI may be celebrated at any time, at the discretion of the individual priest. Usually such a Mass has the Scripture readings in the vernacular, however.

Second, as a result of an indult of Pope John Paul II, the pre-Vatican II rite of the Mass or, more properly, the Mass of Pope St. Pius V (also referred to as the "Tridentine Mass" because it was a product of the reforms of the Council of Trent) may be celebrated with the permission of the local bishop when certain conditions are satisfied: Genuine spiritual need of the petitioners, along with their acceptance of the validity of the new Order of Mass, and no attempt to "politicize" the liturgy of the Church by pitting one rite against the other.

Third, it is possible to have a kind of "hybrid" Mass, in which certain parts are in Latin while others are in the vernacular. Not a few parishes, for example, use Latin for all the sung parts of the Mass. Still others pray the proper parts (those prayers which change from day to day) in the vernacular and the ordinary (unchanging parts) in Latin.

While discussing Latin Masses, it might also be well to address the matter of the direction in which these liturgies may be celebrated. The direction chosen has absolutely nothing to do with the rite used. In the Tridentine Mass, even in the "old days," Mass could be celebrated facing the people. Similarly, in the new Order of Mass, the celebrant may either face East or face the congregation. In fact, the new Roman Missal presumes that the priest is facing East since several rubrics direct him to turn toward the people at given moments for greetings and the like.

The Church of the Latin Rite certainly has a special obligation to preserve, cultivate, and pass on the heritage of the Latin language. The purpose of a Latin liturgy is not to foster nostalgia, much less to serve as a symbol of rebellion against legitimate renewal, but to put and keep Catholics in touch with their roots. As Catholics, we have a unique attachment to the Latin language, which facilitates the much-needed process of "thinking with the Church."

Our Posture in Worship

I T IS THE WHOLE PERSON who adores Almighty God. It is very important that this fact be clear in our worship. If we prayed as disembodied creatures, then our gestures and postures would have no real significance. But someone who is redeemed is completely redeemed—both in body and soul.

This incarnational truth should be apparent when we consider how we pray during the course of the liturgy. In fact, postures and gestures have always been important in worship, among both the Hebrews and other ancient peoples. Hence, the assignment of particular and appropriate postures throughout Mass to engage the entire body in the act of worship. Thus, we show forth externally certain interior attitudes of the heart and mind.

Here are some reflections on postures we adopt at different points during the Sacrifice of the Mass:

- **Standing** is the position of reverent attention, especially during the Gospel and Creed, as well as the ancient posture for the prayer of petition. Thus it is used at the three principal orations or times of petition of the Mass—the Collect, the Prayer over the Gifts, and the Prayer after Communion.

- **Sitting** signifies attentive listening, which is particularly appropriate during the first two readings and the homily.
- **Bowing** may be either profound or simple. A profound bow is made to the altar if the Blessed Sacrament is not reserved on it, while a simple bow is used when uttering the name of Jesus, the Blessed Virgin, or the Pope.
- **Kneeling** symbolizes humble petition and adoration and is therefore used during the Eucharistic Prayer.
- **Genuflection** is the bending of the right knee in adoration of the eucharistic Lord. The priest is required to genuflect to the Blessed Sacrament whenever passing before It during the liturgy, at the elevations of the Lord's Body and Blood during the Consecration, before receiving Holy Communion, and on approaching the tabernacle. The faithful should do so when entering and leaving the church.
- **Raised hands** is the ancient priestly gesture of supplication in the Jewish Tradition. That is why the priest raises his hands at different points throughout the liturgy, especially during the Eucharistic Prayer and the Lord's Prayer.
- **Beating one's breast** is a sign of humility and sorrow for sin and is used during the Confiteor.

Sacred Vestments, Liturgical Colors, and Other Liturgical Objects

SACRED VESTMENTS

P SALM 29 URGES US TO "adore the LORD in holy attire." This command is directed to all the faithful, but in a preeminent manner to those who lead the community in prayer—the priest and his assistants at the altar.

Here is a list of vestments used as "holy attire" in the holy Sacrifice of the Mass:

- The **alb** is a white garment reaching to the ankles. In ancient Rome, it was a tunic. Its name comes from the Latin word for "white."
- The **amice** is a white rectangular garment. Originally, it was worn as a hood, now it is placed about the shoulders, covering the street clothes of the

priest. It is not necessary if the alb is made with a collar, which fulfills the same purpose.

- The **cassock** is the black robe of priests and seminarians, also worn by altar servers. Its color is purple for bishops and monsignori, red for cardinals, and white for the Pope.

- The **chasuble** is *the* eucharistic vestment, worn over the alb and stole. Its color is that of the day. The name is derived from the Latin word for a "little house," a reference to its covering all the other vestments.

- The **cincture** is a cord, either white or the color of the day, which is used to gather the alb at the waist. It is not needed if the alb is made in such a way that this function is already accomplished.

- The **cope** is a full cape or cloak worn by the priest or deacon for solemn celebrations of the sacraments, for processions, and for Benediction of the Blessed Sacrament.

- The **dalmatic** is the outer garment of the deacon, comparable to the chasuble and matching it in color.

- The **humeral veil** is a shawl-like vestment, worn around the shoulders while carrying the Blessed Sacrament in procession or while imparting the eucharistic blessing at Benediction.

- The **maniple** is a napkin-like vestment worn over the left forearm by the priest and deacon in the Tridentine Mass.

- The **mitre** is the tall, two-pointed hat worn by the bishop. It is symbolic of the union of the Old and New Testaments.

- The **pallium** is a woolen garment, resembling a scarf or stole, worn over the chasuble by an archbishop. It symbolizes his authority over an ecclesiastical province and his special union with the Bishop of Rome, from whom he receives the vestment.
- The **stole** is the distinctive sign of one who has received Holy Orders. It is a scarf-like vestment worn by priests under the chasuble or by deacons under the dalmatic, symbolizing the authority to preach and administer the sacraments. Its color is that of the day, matching the chasuble.
- The **surplice** is a white, shirt-like vestment worn over the cassock. It may replace the alb in services other than the Mass.
- The **tunicle** is the outer vestment of the subdeacon in the Tridentine liturgy.
- The **zucchetto** is the skull-cap worn by bishops (purple), cardinals (red), and the pope (white).

LITURGICAL COLORS

In the Latin Rite, five colors are used in the sacred liturgy, which signal particular seasons and feasts:

- **White** is used during Christmastide and Eastertide. It is also used for feasts and memorials of our Lord and our Lady, as well as the angels and saints who were not martyred. Further, it is the color for weddings and baptisms and other occasions of joy. For particularly solemn celebrations, **gold** may be substituted.

- **Red** is used for Passion Sunday (Palm Sunday), Good Friday, and Pentecost. It is also used for days commemorating martyrs since red represents either the blood of martyrs or the fire of God's love.
- **Green**, as the color of growth and new life, is used during the season throughout the year. This season is called Ordinary Time.
- **Violet/Purple** is the color of penance and is thus used for Advent (sometimes a more reddish hue) and Lent. On the Third Sunday of Advent (Gaudete) and the Fourth Sunday in Lent (Laetare), **rose** may replace violet as a call to rejoice in the approaching end of these seasons.
- **Black**, as the color of mourning, may be used for All Souls' Day and for funerals—although in the United States, purple or white are likewise options.

OTHER LITURGICAL OBJECTS

Many other objects are needed for the proper celebration of Mass. Some of them are described below:

- The **altar cloth** is the white covering used for the mensa (table-top) of the altar.
- The **antependium** is a decorative cloth which hangs down in front of the altar, often of the same material as the Mass vestments.

- The **aspergillum** is the container for the holy water, used to sprinkle the congregation, so named from the Latin word for "sprinkle."

- The **burse** is an envelope-like container made of cardboard and covered with cloth of the color of the day, holding the corporal. It is optional in the revised rites but required in the Tridentine Liturgy.

- **Candelabra** are branched candlestick holders, usually for five or seven candles and generally used for eucharistic devotions.

- The **chair** is the seat from which the celebrant presides over the liturgy. It should not resemble the bishop's throne, which is called a **cathedra,** and hence, the name of "cathedral" for a bishop's church.

- The **chalice** is the cup which contains the precious Blood and should, therefore, be of some precious metal, which is neither porous nor fragile.

- The **chalice veil,** of the same material as the Mass vestments or else white, covers the chalice until it is brought to the altar at the Preparation of the Gifts.

- The **ciborium** is another vessel of precious metal. It holds the hosts for the reception of the faithful. Its name comes from the Latin word for "food," holding as it does the "Bread of Life." It is kept in the *tabernacle,* the ark-like container which holds the Blessed Sacrament for purposes of Communion to the sick and adoration. Its name is derived from the Latin word for "tent"—a reminder of the meeting tent of the ancient Hebrews where

God's glory dwelt in their midst.

- The **corporal** is a square of linen folded into nine parts, on which the paten and chalice rest during the Liturgy of the Eucharist. It received its name from the Latin "corpus," which refers to the Body of the Lord.

- The **crucifix** is the cross with the body of our Savior on it. Every sanctuary must have a crucifix present for the celebration of Mass, in order to offer a visible reminder of the connection between the Eucharistic Sacrifice and Christ's self-oblation on Calvary.

- **Cruets** are the containers for the water and wine, usually made of glass, so that the wine and water can be readily distinguished.

- The **finger towel** is a small cloth used to dry the celebrant's hands after washing them.

- The **lectern, pulpit** or **ambo** is the stand from which the Scripture readings are proclaimed and the homily is delivered. There should only be one of these in the sanctuary, from which the entire Liturgy of the Word is conducted to signify the unity of the Word. No other activities should take place at this stand. If a place is needed for a cantor, a simple music stand should be used.

- The **lectionary** is the book which contains all the Scripture readings. Ideally, a separate *Book of the Gospels* should be used by the priest or deacon for the proclamation of the Gospel.

- The **luna** is the glass container which holds the

large Host placed in the monstrance for adoration; it is called this because it resembles a moon (*luna* in Latin).

- The **monstrance** or **ostensorium** is the vessel in which the Blessed Sacrament is placed for exposition, procession, and blessing, so named since both words in Latin mean "to show."
- The **pall** is a cardboard square covered with linen and sometimes embroidered used to cover the chalice, particularly to keep out particles of dust or insects. The cloth placed over the casket during the Mass of Christian Burial is also called a pall.
- The **paten** is the plate on which the host rests, likewise made of a precious metal. It may also refer to the plate held by the altar boy under the communicant's chin during the distribution of Holy Communion, to catch a Host, should It fall from the priest's hand.
- The **purificator** is a cloth used to dry the sacred vessels after their purification.
- The **pyx** is a small ciborium, generally used to bring Holy Communion to the sick.
- The **Roman Missal** is the book of all the official prayers of the Mass, as well as the General Instruction which provides all the necessary directives to celebrate Mass. In some places it is referred to as a *sacramentary.*
- The **thurible** is a metal bowl hanging by one or three chains, which holds the charcoal and incense.

Questions for Group Discussion for Appendices

1. According to the Second Vatican Council, what is the place of Latin in the liturgy?

2. Note some of the advantages of using Latin more extensively than most parishes in the United States presently do. Discuss.

3. How would you answer the objection that all the various postures used for Mass have no real significance and simply complicate worship?

4. What is the rationale behind having the priest vested in special garb reserved only for the liturgy?

5. Given all the poverty in the world, might the Church not be more pleasing to God, if she gave up beautiful church buildings, vestments, and vessels—in favor of sharing this wealth with the poor? Discuss.